D0064761

CROSSCURRENTS *Modern Critiques*

CROSSCURRENTS *Modern Critiques*
Harry T. Moore, *General Editor*

Charles I. Glicksberg

The Tragic Vision

IN TWENTIETH-CENTURY LITERATURE

WITH A PREFACE BY

Harry T. Moore

SOUTHERN ILLINOIS UNIVERSITY PRESS
Carbondale and Edwardsville

FEFFER & SIMONS, INC.
London and Amsterdam

PREFACE

THE REDUCTION OF MAN has resulted in a reduction of what Charles I. Glicksberg writes of as the tragic vision. Mr. Glicksberg carefully shows how the concept of tragedy has had to fight for its life among various recent philosophies or attitudes such as Marxism, Existentialism, and scientific rationalism. His study is of particular value because of its detailed consideration of the subject; he doesn't leave generalities hanging, but shows specifically and emphatically how the statements he makes applies to various authors and their work.

Tragedy, as he points out, is an affirmation; hence the nihilistic, the purposeless, and the absurd, all prevalent today, can not be genuinely tragic. Mr. Glicksberg begins his survey with Kierkegaard, father of so much modern philosophy. Kierkegaard's faith, Mr. Glicksberg shows, did not embody tragic vision, although Kiergegaard's own life was, ironically, tragic in itself. Mr. Glicksberg goes on to examine the doctrines of Nietzsche, Kafka, Sartre, and others, as well as Marxian and scientific influences.

Occasionally Mr. Glicksberg agrees with the findings of George Steiner, whose own brilliant investigation of the subject, The Death of Tragedy, was published in 1961; but Mr. Glicksberg is sometimes in opposition to Mr. Steiner, as when he says that "the new form of tragedy is not only possible in our time; it has been produced by such men as Faulkner, Malraux, O'Neill, Sartre, and Camus." These are writers who have accepted Nietzsche's premise that God is dead, but have nevertheless found ways to express the tragic vision, often in defiance of the meaningless or the absurd.

It must be stressed that, for the most part, the Steiner and Glicksberg books do not cover the same ground. In the larger themes, the determination of what is and is not tragic, they often deal with the same topics, but essentially they treat different historic periods. Both books make only token references to the Greeks; Mr. Steiner, however, treats Corneille and Racine in detail, and gives Byron's tragic dramas a significant new emphasis. But Mr. Steiner gives only a quick glance at contemporary writers. Mr. Glicksberg provides no extensive examination of works of the far past but, as his title promises, he does give close attention to more recent writers. Hence his book and Mr. Steiner's are essentially complementary.

Mr. Glicksberg goes along with George Steiner in believing that neither Marxism nor Christianity can foster tragedy, yet in a fine chapter on "Malraux and the Myth of Violence," Mr. Glicksberg skillfully shows how Marxist subject matter can come within the range of the tragic vision. The Marxist state does not encourage tragedy because it is built upon an enforced optimism which rules out this tragic vision; but the plight of individual revolutionaries can be tragic, like that of Kyo in Man's Fate. This novel, Mr. Glicksberg says, "is the carrier of the tragic vision in that it affirms an ethic of human responsibility, the will to human dignity, in the face of the incurable absurdity of existence." But, as Mr. Glicksberg further points out, this "revolutionary novel par excellence" contains "implications that make it anti-Marxist in content." He then proceeds to unravel these complications.

But why can not some of these same points be made, in effect, about Christianity? That is, why must the implications of Christianity be necessarily non-tragic? Granted, Christianity is, like Marxism, officially a doctrine of optimism: with the possibility of salvation always within range, the hero should properly arrive at a happy ending, certainly an untragic one. But what of the hero who fails—is he not tragic? This was an issue I raised in discussing George Steiner's book in the Kenyon Review (Summer 1961): "Perhaps a ritual Christian drama would perforce sing happiness and conclude with a Paradiso; but what of non-official plays, such as Shakespeare's, which were after all written in a Christian culture? Shakespeare's heroes often fall into the catastrophe of the tragic because they violate community imperatives not always necessarily Christian in origin, though adaptably so. The very prospect of a paradisal reward intensifies, in non-Calvinist Christianity, the tragic element: it emphasizes the hero's personal responsibility as it underlines his failure."

One of the values of such books as Mr. Glicksberg's, as of Mr. Steiner's, is that it can keep such questions going. Altogether, The Tragic Vision in Twentieth-Century Literature is an important investigation of one of the great literary and human subjects, which it treats with thoroughness. Further, its insights are continually helpful; they will enrich the literary awareness of its readers.

HARRY T. MOORE

University of Colorado
December 6, 1962

NOTE

It is good to see Charles I. Glickberg's book going into another printing. The volume has been most cordially received.

H.T.M.

Southern Illinois University
September 11, 1968

CONTENTS

INTRODUCTION

A NUMBER OF CRITICS are at present puzzled and disturbed by the fact that the modern age has given birth to no impressive examples of the tragic form, none that can compare with the achievement of the ancient Greek and Elizabethan writers. Over and over again writers have preferred the charge, as if it were a shameful lack in our culture, that ours is indeed not a tragic age. Oswald Spengler delivers a characteristic magisterial judgment in *The Decline of the West*. Joseph Wood Krutch, in *The Modern Temper*, argues cogently that the scientific revolution has reduced man to atomistic insignificance, preventing that affirmation of the greatness of the human soul which is the indispensable basis of tragedy. George Steiner, in *The Death of Tragedy*, insists eloquently that tragedy is dead. He even denies the possibility of the restoration of tragic drama. The assumption that it is impossible to produce tragedy in the twentieth century has become a fixed conviction.

Naturalistic in outlook, the modern drama, it is said, reflects a type of life that is characterized by industrialized regimentation and by the supremacy of the scientific philosophy that interprets man as the victim of determinism. In its fidelity to the verisimilitude of the commonplace, it presents marginal, inarticulate characters who lack the greatness of soul that marked the tragic art of the past. The reliance on the factors of heredity and environment as the determinants of fate denies them the freedom of choice that is basic to the tragic conflict. If man is portrayed as shaped inevitably by a complex of economic, environmental, and hereditary forces, he cannot take on the traits of the heroic. Even in his neurotic afflictions, as in the work of Strindberg and Tennessee Williams, he appears often as pathetic and abnormal, deprived of moral autonomy. According to Erich Fromm in *Escape from Freedom,* by suppressing his awareness of the reality of death, modern man loses the sense of tragedy.[1] The conclusion to be drawn from all this is supposed to be inescapable: the tradition of tragedy inaugurated in Greece two thousand five hundred years ago is practically extinct.

It is hard to comprehend why this must be so. Men suffer today as excruciatingly as they did in Athens in the fifth century before Christ, though they view their suffering from a radically different philosophical perspective. Heirs of the Age of Enlightenment, they have reached a point where they realize that in ultimate matters the scientific method and the uses of reason cannot help them to solve the riddle of existence. The conquest of matter and space, the splitting of the atom, the triumph of technology, the stupendous successes achieved by the application of the scientific method, have resulted, paradoxically enough, in a situation where man today confronts the specter of meaninglessness. His attempt, since the time of Bacon, to search out the secrets of Nature, has shattered his former confidence in rational laws.[2] Twentieth-century man has ceased to believe in the reality of the invisible world. For him there is no life after death.[3] Christianity has been found to be ineffectual in averting the fate of annihilation that threatens to overwhelm all mankind. For the majority of Europeans, Camus declares, "faith is lost." [4]

It will be our task in this book to ascertain whether the modern age has not given rise to new forms of the tragic vision.[5] Neither the Greek nor Shakespearean tragic forms can, it is true, find embodiment on the stage today, since the world image or the religious faith out of which they grew is no longer shared by the Western audience. That community of belief which enabled the Greek or Elizabethan hero to face his destiny with high-hearted courage is no longer available to us on the old terms. The contemporary imagination, nourished on the scientific synthesis and haunted by anticipations of global disaster, cannot recapture the spontaneous vitality assured by the myths of the past. Our civilization has evolved new and different myths. We live in an age of ideologies, political mystiques, and atomic armaments. No law of justice, human or divine, reigns supreme. If catastrophe strikes, it will not be brought about by the wrath of the gods or the cruelty of fate but by the blunders of history.

There is thus a profound difference between the *Weltanschauung* of the Greek tragic writers and that which informs those works of our age which are instinct with the tragic vision. The modern tragic hero is still at the mercy of alien and unpredictable forces, the human condition still remains ambiguous, but he is now convinced that no final explanation of the mystery of existence is possible.[6] No longer believing in heaven or hell, he has ceased to search for rational justification. Like Dionysus in Euripides' *Bacchae,* he discerns no law of equivalence between the punishment inflicted on man and his presumptive guilt. Science, which set out to establish the sovereign sway of universal laws, discovers no hint of moral meaning or purpose in the cosmos. If standards of good and evil exist at all, they are present in man alone. On him now falls the full responsibility for creating his own pattern of order and meaning in Nature.

Science, as it disclosed the inexorable limits of human knowledge, did not silence the voice of the tragic vision; it simply compelled it to speak a new language. No definition of tragedy or the tragic vision can be made so all-inclusive as to overcome all objections that might be raised. *"There is simply no single true philosophy of tragedy,"* John Gassner declares, *"any more than there is a single inviolable tragic form."* [7] Gassner contends that the modern age has, in fact, produced a number of plays which qualify as tragedies, even if they do not resemble the august tragedies of the past. He cites such plays as *Ghosts, Hedda Gabler, The Father, The Power of Darkness, The Lower Depths, The Hairy Ape, Desire Under the Elms, Mourning Becomes Electra,* and *The Iceman Cometh* as evidence supporting his thesis. He sees no reason why rationalism and social realism based on verisimilitude must spell the death of tragedy. From this he proceeds to the curious *non sequitur* that tragedy could be legitimately denounced as "lack of faith, as antisocial defeatism, or as the vain indulgence of morbidity in periods of moral reformation." [8]

This interpretation of the problem of tragedy by a liberal critic runs counter to the conception of the tragic vision set forth in this book. The authentic tragic vision is committed to no program of social optimism; it demonstrates the ineffectuality of all temporal and historical remedies. It recognizes that man is responsible to himself alone, but it also reveals the terrible burden of suffering he must bear that no secular reforms will remove. Life remains inexplicable and calamitous today as in the past, though for different reasons. The tragic protagonist knows that his suffering and shipwreck is not caused by the evils of society or the pressures of economics. Murray Krieger attacks the literary naturalists as men of little heart, naïve in their belief in the salvationary value of social morality and social progress. Evading "the atheist's existential obligation to confront nothingness in its frighteningly empty consequences," they "construct elaborate rational structures based on nothingness," whistling "in the dark as if all were light." [9]

The literary naturalists of our time who have given voice to the tragic vision suffer from no such cheerful illusions. They present no optimistic resolution of the conflict inherent in the human condition. The tragic visionary in the work of Malraux, Sartre, O'Neill, and Camus comes at last to the knowledge that his pride of reason cannot save him; the order of the universe is not at all concerned with his destiny. Nor does he look forward to some utopian consummation in the future which will save the children of Adam from the catastrophe which overtakes him. When the chips are down, he perceives that the universe utterly fails to conform to the reasons of the heart or of the mind. It is this envisagement of the human condition which, in different ways, is to be found in the writings of such men as Kafka, Céline, Hemingway, Samuel Beckett, Strindberg, and Gottfried Benn.

Though the modern tragic vision affirms no principle of moral or spiritual transcendence, it does exhibit the drama of unjustified and unrelieved suffering. Though the tragic visionary catches no glimpse of significance that would redeem his suffering, he is not without a measure of greatness when he is brought face to face with disaster. Kyo, the professional revolutionist in *Man's Fate*, accepts his death as a sacrifice in order to defend the dignity of the lowest classes of mankind. Dr. Rieux, in *The Plague*, is a protagonist who asserts the need for human solidarity and infinite compassion precisely because there is no supernatural power to whom man can turn for aid. It is only when the dramatist blames society for the misfortunes that befall the victim, as Arthur Miller does in *Death of a Salesman*, that we get the grim pathos of social realism rather than tragic exaltation. The tragic hero, even as he suffers defeat, acknowledges that sense of overriding mystery which O'Neill sought to capture in *The Hairy Ape*, *Beyond the Horizon*, and *The Great God Brown*: "the mystery any man or woman can feel but not understand as the meaning of any event—or accident—in any life on earth. And it is this mystery I want to realize in the theatre." [10]

The tragic vision, however ambiguous or "negative" in content, endeavors at all times to communicate the meaning of this mystery. It is the imaginative record of the attempt, usually despairing but never abandoned, to discern some pattern of justice in the ways of fate. Even the perception of absurdity as the final meaning of the human adventure on earth culminates, in the work of Malraux,

Camus, and Sartre, in an existential decision to abide by those values which man himself has chosen. Life may be a naturalistic chaos, but the tragic hero seeks to uphold his identity even though he can do nothing about his condition. His struggle and suffering take on meaning, even if they cannot be justified. His struggle is the measure of his greatness, for "as long as he struggles against the dark, death, and evil, he holds them off, and for every moment that they are held off, he has succeeded." [11] These are the paradoxes and polarities that are fused in the dialectics of the tragic vision.

Defiantly secular, literary nihilism affirms only the necessity for revolt against the human condition. It beholds in the spectacle of suffering a supreme example, one of many, of the meaninglessness of existence. Upholder of the Nietzschean faith in the aesthetic resolution of the mystery of being, Gottfried Benn, the nihilist par excellence, turns to art as his last defence. Nihilism, he concludes, is inevitable in the twentieth century. The white race is not only declining but doomed. He is close to the tragic vision in his belief that modern art testifies to the disappearance of all meaning. He could not transcend his nihilism. Literature for him was but one of the drugs that made life bearable.[12]

Though the dominant mood of modern literature of the tragic vision is nihilistic, it does what Gottfried Benn failed to do: it protests against the absence of justice in the universe. It portrays fate as blind and contingent, but it voices the universal motif of compassion for the human lot. That is the characteristic note struck in the work of the writers who are discussed in this book. They believe that the meaning of life is life itself. They do not find any law of moral equivalence governing human affairs. Suffering is intolerably heightened because it is no longer seen as justified. It strikes at random and affects everyone, without bringing any redemptive wisdom.

Some critics maintain that tragedy must come to a dead end if the writer discerns no such moral balance at work.[13] Obviously if the tragic vision must affirm hope, then those nihilistic novels and dramas which are rooted in the myth of meaninglessness are not tragic. Life must at all costs be affirmed, even if the writer is convinced that it corresponds to no principle of justice. But this is precisely what the tragic vision of our time tries to do. What does the tragic protagonist, from Ahab in *Moby Dick* to Goetz in *The Devil and the Good Lord*, defend if not the sacredness and preciousness of life. He dies unreconciled, continuing to protest against an absurdity that he recognizes as unalterable. He refuses to fool himself. He faces life honestly, and not without irony, no matter how appalling the truth turns out to be. He expects no reward and no vindication for the suffering he is forced to undergo. Thus he is not at all of the persuasion "that every tragedy is a demonstration of the justice of the unalterable conditions of human experience." [14] On the contrary, the tragic vision, as it explores the kingdom of nothingness, abandons all illusion. But however darkly "negative" its conclusions may seem to be, it nevertheless affirms the value of life itself. The work of art is in itself a denial of the myth of nothingness. [15]

To create is to affirm, even if all that the work affirms is the impenetrable mystery that cradles all of existence. The twentieth-century tragic protagonist, heroic or not, learns to accept his finite limitations in an incomprehensible universe, but he does not cease from mental fight. What generates the tension of inner conflict is his refusal to believe that his life is ruled completely by the blind dicemen of contingency. He asserts his freedom and seeks to discover who he is. This is the nature of the paradox that is embodied in the tragic vision of our century.

Kierkegaard, Nietzsche, and Kafka are the three prophets, each in his own way, of nihilistic absurdity. By taking "the leap" into faith, Kierkegaard escapes the consequences of dread and despair that the vision of the infinite absurd induces, but the religious solution he advocates precludes the birth of tragedy. Hailing the death of God, Nietzsche spells out all the metaphysical implications to be drawn from a God-abandoned world. He is our key figure of Promethean defiance, the instigator of the modern revolt. It is he who, at the start of our inquiry, best illustrates the difficulties that attend the modern writer's effort to derive the tragic vision from nihilistic premises. In the case of Kafka, the impossibility of either affirming or rejecting life reaches a climax of ambiguity. The absurd is enthroned. Camus, like Sartre, transcends the myth of Sisyphus by showing how man can live in a universe that is without ultimate meaning.

Tragedy is neither philosophy nor ideology, but the writer today dwells in a world in which ideas are living forces that influence the attitudes of men and affect the destiny of society. Malraux introduces a gallery of characters all of whom suffer from some form of mythomania. The Russian nihilists of the nineteenth century accepted materialism, atheism, and the mystique of the peasant as their new "religion." The contributions of Marx, Darwin, Freud, and Einstein have revolutionized the conception men have of themselves and of their place in the universe. Ideology enters into the structure of the tragic vision as part of the outlook characteristic of the hero, the interpretation he gives of himself. In the second part of this book we attempt to analyze the impact on modern literature of science, Marxism, psychoanalysis, and Existentialism. Our object is to show concretely how the literary consciousness of the twentieth century expresses its tragic vision of life in a universe that no longer bears the intolerable shadow of God's presence.

Nihilism and Tragedy

1   THE PROBLEM OF TRAGEDY
IN THE TWENTIETH CENTURY

TWENTIETH-CENTURY LITERATURE GIVES expression to a complex, interwoven theme of Promethean defiance and Sisyphean despair. The motifs of rebellion and fatalism, mechanical necessity and human freedom, coexist in a dialectic which the modern creative mind seems unable to resolve. These are the irreconcilable conflicts and contradictions that we shall encounter at every turn in our study of the tragic vision. They form a pattern of irony, ambivalent and paradoxical, which holds up for inspection mutually antagonistic points of view and rejects all of them as untenable and absurd. The evangel of nihilism that Nietzsche prophetically proclaimed in the last quarter of the nineteenth century has vanquished the realm of the sacred. Literary nihilism portrays man as a biological creature of instinct who nevertheless possesses a consciousness that enables him to discover the secrets of Nature and rebel against all those dark powers that militate against life and negate his own humanity.

Frequently the nihilistic hero, for all his pride of rebellion, has nothing to live *for* and his only solution, therefore, is, like a Stavrogin or a Kirillov, to take his own life. Quentin Compson, in *The Sound and the Fury*, feels that all he has sought and suffered is denied significance. His mind recalls the lesson in disillusionment his alcoholic father had taught him, "that all men are just dolls stuffed with sawdust swept up from the trash heaps where all previous dolls had been thrown away the sawdust flowing from what wounds in what side that not for me died not." [1] The Man on the Cross had not died for Quentin, and that is because every human being is under the iron sway of necessity. The strange thing, Quentin recalls his father saying, is that man, conceived by accident, "whose every breath is a fresh cast with dice already loaded against him," will not face the truth of death until he comes to realize that even his despair or remorse or bereavement "is not particularly important to the dark dicemen." [2] The gods, the dark dicemen, the agents of the biological will that Hardy ironically calls "It," have us completely in their power. Men must bear the terrible burden of pain and death without any justification for their struggle and their suffering on earth.

The Sound and the Fury offers a striking illustration of the difference in meaning between the tragic forms of the past and the tragic vision of the present. The difference is to be found in what the tragic hero *sees* as he is about to suffer shipwreck. Though the Greek hero, an Oedipus, can do nothing to avert his fate, he is under the governance of the all-powerful gods. Whereas Oedipus, when he learns the truth about himself, resigns himself to the will of the gods, the modern hero goes down to defeat in a world that seems cruel and purposeless. Frederick Henry, as he sits in the hospital waiting for news of his Catherine who had just given birth to a dead child, reflects defiantly: One died without knowing what it was all about. [3] He recalls how once in camp he put a log on top of the fire and watched how the ants scurried frantically and ran toward the center where the fire burned and then fled back toward the end and finally fell off into the flames. [4] For Hemingway, the fiery immolation of the ants presents a frightening symbol of the end of the world. The modern hero beholds a vision, instinct with irony, of a life that is without meaning and beyond redemption.

This marks at least the starting point of the tragic vision: the recognition of the meaninglessness of life, which is counterbalanced by the ever-present need to affirm the greatness of the human spirit that can face up to its destiny, whatever it be. In thus demonstrating man's capacity to endure with courage the worst that life in its malice can inflict, the tragic vision rises above the vicissitudes of time-bound circumstances and the blind cruelty of fate. Rooted as it is in the ambiguity of the human condition, the tragic vision constitutes an affirmation, however "negative" or equivocal in content, of the greatness of man as he confronts the ultimate meaning of existence, which may be an utter absence of meaning. It is this "mad" persistence in the impossible quest for meaning that is the vital and enduring element in the tragic vision.

It is a vision that dispenses with the illusion of hope. The Chorus in *Antigone* voices Anouilh's conception of tragedy. "There isn't any hope. You're trapped. The whole sky has fallen on you, and all you can do about it is to shout." [5] All the modern tragic hero can do about his trapped condition is to shout aloud and say all those things "that you never thought you'd be able to say—or never even knew you had it in you to say. And you don't say these things because it will do any good to say them: you know better than that. You say them for their own sake." [6] That is how Anouilh brings out the basic distinction between melodrama and tragedy; in the latter there is no possibility of escape; all argument or protest is gratuitous.

ii

Though literature is part of a continuing tradition, with its established genres, structures, and styles, the tradition undergoes marked changes in the course of time. In the theater, for example, the language of poetry gives way to that of prose. It is hard to conceive of *Ghosts* or *A Doll's House* or even *The Wild Duck* composed in sonorous blank verse or heroic couplets. These changes of style and structure, these shifts from tragedy to tragicomedy, not to mention the replacement in popular appeal of the drama by the novel, are to be accounted for in large measure by a radical transformation in the consciousness and sensibility of an age. When the world view is suddenly disturbed violently, when things fall apart and the center cannot hold and "Mere anarchy is loosed upon the world," the writer is forced to experiment with new forms of expression. The old bottles cannot hold the new fermenting wine. Such a radical transformation of the world image took place in post-Enlightenment thought from 1750 to 1960.[7]

In the space of approximately two centuries, man turned from angel into ape, from spirit into commodity. The Age of Enlightenment sought to deny the contingent and extrude the problematical from the equation of life. It set out to conquer Nature and make it conform to the rules of reason and order. Inheritors of the cosmology and the conception of man derived from Descartes, Locke, and Hobbes, the eighteenth-century philosophers pictured the universe as a machine governed by a First Cause. Man, too, was regarded as a machine. What could not be empirically confirmed was to be rejected. Reason was to reign supreme.

But reason visited its revenge upon its devotees. Knowledge and reason both proved inadequate. The split between intellect and intuition, mind and spirit, objectivity and subjectivity, deepened. Escaped from their lairs in the underground of the psyche, the demons of the irrational abolished all the symmetrical constructions of logic. The truth of the human condition, in all its existential contradictions, emerged. No longer satisfied with the old explanations, man stood alone before a Nature that is alien. He ceased to be able to understand Nature and felt, as Rilke says, "that it was the Other, indifferent towards men."[8] Rationalism gave way to Existentialism. Kierkegaard waged war against the Hegelian system of abstractions. The secret self became hauntingly aware of its finiteness and contingency. Man saw himself now as a divided being, at one with Nature and yet apart from it. His spirit demanded the bread of life that science alone could not satifsy. Under the scientific dispensation, man was turned into a victim, pathetically sorry for himself but unable to do anything about his condition. In a startling image that opens the story, "The Metamorphosis," Kafka describes a new demonic process of zoological transformation—Gregor Samsa awakens from uneasy dreams to find himself changed into a gigantic insect—which effectually negates the sphere of the sacred.[9] The only weapon with which the modern writer can combat this oppressive sense of the victimization of man is to view the human condition from the perspective of irony sharpened by his rebellious consciousness.

The spirit of irony is today woven into the fabric of the tragic vision. Refusing to be deluded by romantic utopianism, the cult of progress, the dream of human perfectibility, the tragic vision responded to Nietzsche's call for laughter. It sought to arrive at its own understanding of the unavoidable frustrations and limitations of life: what is possible and what is forever impossible. Such insights intensified the value of laughter.[10] The tragic view of life was now incorporated with the comic vein, the sense of the absurd.[11]

The difficulties that stand in the way of creating tragedy in the twentieth century grew in large part out of the problem that arose when men in increasing numbers ceased to believe in the existence of God and in the moral values that were supported by the Christian doctrine. If nihilism is the unavoidable condition of man today (and by "nihilism" we simply mean a state of mind which realizes that God is dead and that man, liberated from the bondage of religious or moral authority, is "free" to make himself in a universe that remains alien [12]), the obstacles that block the release of the tragic vision are formidable but not insuperable. If man does not know the answer to the metaphysical questions his mind persists in asking, he is not thereby disqualified from shouting aloud all those things he never knew he had it in him to say. He must act, though never certain that his choice is the right one or what the consequences of his choice will be. So long as he consents to life—and he does so consent, at least on the biological plane—he must somehow come to terms with existence. The tragic outlook, however defiant in temper, must affirm, if only by implication, the a priori value of life itself.

Beginning with Nietzsche, this is precisely what literary nihilists of our age have tried to do. They voice a tragic humanism that upholds the courage and dignity of man in his foiled quest for meaning. His noblest endeavors are destined to fail, but he does not for that reason give up the struggle, even if it is waged without "that foul, deceitful thing," hope.[13] The nihilistic spokesmen of our time perceive the absurd as a haunting, pervasive, almost numinous presence, but they will not call it God. What kind of God would this personified absurdity turn out to be? A strictly negative God, an incarnation of absence, a symbol of the emptiness of the sky, a God deaf, dumb, and blind, a reminder of the senselessness of all human projects. Facing up to the fact of their orphaned state in the universe, they will not silence the protesting, if ineffectual, voice of reason or prostrate themselves before inscrutable powers. That is why their attempts at tragic utterance are shot through with overtones not only of irony but metaphysical revolt.

Rebelling against the tyranny of time, the absurdity of his lot, the ignominy of death, the modern hero as victim achieves no culminating moment of transfiguration or redemption. Despite his victimized state, he is a "rebel" in that, like Orestes in *The Flies*, he has no further use for the gods. In the archetypal struggle against necessity, he is bound to lose, but it is this very knowledge that leads him to rebel against his fate. Neither villain nor saint, he looks upon himself as a victim who has chosen to revolt. He exists, therefore he rebels: that is the mark of his humanity.[14] It is this demonic element in his nature that spurs him on to undertake a quest that is essentially, if negatively, "religious" in character. Primarily what he rebels against is the contingency of existence, the abyss of absurdity into which his nihilistic *Weltanschauung* plunges him.

iii

Thus man, not Nature, becomes the sole source of whatever meaning can be elicited. It is through the mediating work of art that he confronts, without illusion, life in all its threatening, terrible aspects. When caught up on the crest of the tragic moment, he stands alone, beholding reality in its disclosure of the appalling and yet exhilarating truth. When his ship strikes a rock and is about to go down, there is no perception on his part that good will triumph over evil, no overriding effect of poetic justice. I. A. Richards states the case incisively: "Tragedy is only possible to a mind which is for the moment agnostic or Manichaean. The least touch of any theology which has a compensating Heaven to offer the tragic hero is fatal." [15]

Gone are the eternal moral laws, gone is the religious faith that once sustained man in his "trials" and tribulations on earth. Gone, too, is the belief in heaven and hell, angels and demons, God and Devil, grace, original sin, immortality, and redemption. Profoundly influenced by the scientific revolution which began in the seventeenth century and which came to a head in the second half of the nineteenth, the cosmology of the modern writer pictures a neutral universe of energy and process in which man feels not only estranged but *de trop*. The dazzling visions of utopian progress that the young hero of "Locksley Hall" beholds as he dips into the future, have turned into terrifying premonitions of atomic disaster. The nineteenth-century romantic dreamer, for all his impatience with the slow, creeping pace of scientific advance, doubts not that "thro' the ages one increasing purpose runs." It is this very sense of purpose that the modern mind, skeptical and Manichaean, is forced to reject.

Such nihilism seems at first glance to undermine the possibility of communicating the tragic vision. It catches no hint of meaning in the throbbing expenditure of energy in space, the furious cycles of creation and destruction and renewal which exemplify the workings of the blind biological will. This is the scientific "myth" that holds the modern mind captive but by which it is nevertheless constrained to live.[16] Thomas Hardy foreshadows the pessimism that pervades the poetry of Robinson Jeffers and the naturalistic plays of Eugene O'Neill. In "Nature's Questioning," he has the objects of Nature ask:

> Has some Vast Imbecility,
>   Mighty to build and blend,
>   But impotent to tend,
> Framed us in jest, and left us now to hazardry?

The question provides its own mordant, inconsolable answer. This is at bottom the absurdist feeling of "nausea" that Sartre makes much of, the vista of Nothingness that Heidegger explores, the Inhumanism that Jeffers preaches as his gospel of "salvation."

Unlike Hardy, Jeffers does not feel that Nature is going anywhere. For all we can tell, it is going nowhere. Evolution is not progress. The only logical future for the human species is extinction. With inspired lyrical eloquence Jeffers praises the beauty of nonbeing. The philosophical attitude that he calls Inhumanism involves "a shifting of emphasis from man to not-man; the rejection of human solipsism and recognition of the transhuman significance." [17] Mankind must give up its crazed attachment to things human and finite. This is not pessimism or misanthropy, Jeffers declares, but a courageous way of facing the truth. Nonetheless, the belief that annihilation offers the only road to "freedom" for mankind, falls short of or goes beyond the limits of the tragic vision, which is never reconciled to the myth of Nirvana. Jeffers beholds no trace of nobility in the actions of men; human beings are the microbes infecting a miniscule satellite caught in the whirlwind of a world of stars.

Jeffers is the modern Cassandra prophetically announcing the doom of humanity. The motif of death looms large in a technological civilization that gloomily anticipates its own extinction. [18] The cruel fate of dissolution, that is the obsession to which a nihilistic novelist like Céline is committed in *Journey to the End of the Night*. The molecules of which the flesh is composed want to fall apart, to escape the bondage of the body, to lose themselves as soon as possible in the universe of matter. The biological ignominy that awaits all men is to be packed off, like so much refuse, to the cemetery.

Albert Camus also looks upon death as the enemy. It is the intrusion of death that transformed this planet into a prison so that the human longing for happiness turned into a curse. Since the lease on life may be ended abruptly by the coming of death, the crime of crimes, according to Camus, is to become resigned to this humiliating condition. This is the dualism which afflicts modern man and which lies at the base of his tragic vision: his hunger for life without end is overshadowed by the knowledge that he must die. Death, by rendering life absurd, forces man to question whether life is worth having. But powerless as reason is to deal with a world that is a chaos of contradictions, Camus contends that the absurd must be borne, even when one rebels against it. The metaphysical rebel spurns the religious opiate of hope. There is nothing beyond the earth, no justification for converting into an object of faith that which lies beyond the range of human awareness. The world is meaningless. Facing the ultimate indignity of death, the writer revolts by affirming life in the present. If art, even in its expression of revolt, is compounded of illusion, it is the only kind of illusion that keeps faith with the universe of the absurd.

Camus's work, which we shall analyze in a later chapter, demonstrates that the absurd in itself is not enough to sustain the tragic vision. The absurd is antitragic not because it jettisons the promise of eternity but because it deprives man of the freedom to revolt against his destiny. Camus had read both Kierkegaard and Heidgger. He knew that while Nothingness may be an active metaphysical force that drives home the reality of human finitude, it cannot be presented as a living character in drama or fiction.[19] The tragic vision cannot emerge in a universe that man knows to be irremediably absurd. In *The Rebel*, Camus declares that metaphysical rebellion is a justified protest against the incompleteness of human life. The metaphysical rebel is a blasphemer who denounces God "as the origin of death and as the supreme disillusionment."[20] He is saddled with the responsibility of creating the order and justice that the reign of God had failed to establish.

The metaphysical rebel of the twentieth century detects the cosmic imposture and revolts against it, but he knows that this changes nothing.[21] Not in the slightest degree is the absurdity of existence affected by the perception that it is absurd. By persevering in the effort to communicate the absurd truth of life, the writer affirms that art at least is a meaningful activity. The tragic vision today is thus instinct with the fearful mystery of meaninglessness that cradles all of existence, but it also pays tribute to the grandeur of man and his unique gift of consciousness that sets him apart from Nature. Nothingness may be, for Heidegger, a living presence that haunts human consciousness, but it is not a viable creative principle. The writer cannot derive nourishment from the source of non-being. Since there is no world beyond, man must, as Camus insists, make his finite experience an end in itself. It is this acceptance of the necessity for revolt, even though it falls invariably short of the goal, that makes it possible for the writer to provide some resolution, however paradoxical, of the tragic conflict.

The modern tragic spirit reflects what we have described as the impossible truth of the human condition. It harps on the inevitability of suffering and on the fact of death as an obscene breach of justice. An absurdist turned rebel, the twentieth-century hero raises the ontological questions basic to all tragedy: why suffering must be woven into the warp and woof of experience, why Nature conforms to no rational order that he can comprehend, why death reigns. In the course of this study we shall see how the modern writer struggles to embody the tragic vision even though he is convinced that suffering, like death, is senseless. This takes us to the heart of the matter. In this *Götterdämmerung* of the West, the mark of the great man, according to Gottfried Benn, is his commitment to nihilism. His creative work shadows forth the void, the inhuman element against which the frail human being is pitted. From Dostoevski to Céline, the human spirit is convulsed

> in an attitude of sheer despair, its screams more terrible, more agonized, more evil than ever were the screams of men condemned to die. These screams are of a moral nature, definite in meaning, they are substantial and always 'against' something, at war 'with' something, struggling 'for' something, trying to include 'everything' and to remain honest, to improve, to complete, to purify, to deify. They are Lutherian screams in a Faustian skirmish. . . . Only today, before so much absurdity and torment, we dimly discern that life is not meant to gain possession of knowledge, and man, at any rate the higher-developed race, is not meant to struggle for an explanation of the material world.[22]

Nihilism, in short, is inevitable. These Lutherian screams in a Faustian skirmish are silenced when modern man realizes that he can never penetrate the secret of the universe. This, then, is the categorical law: "Nothing is, if anything ever was; nothing will be." [23]

The idea of anarchy, however, runs counter to the triumph of order that is fundamental to art. As Una Ellis-Fermor points out in *The Frontiers of Drama,* if writers were to work on the principle that chaos constitutes the ultimate nature of the universe (and that is the assumption basic to the nihilistic literature of our age), they could not express this vision in dramatic or fictional terms. The paradox remains: "how achieve the revelation of formlessness in the strict artistic forms?" [24] This is the paradox that bedevils those novelists and dramatists who try to impose some viable pattern of meaning on the chaotic flux of experience. The borderline which separates art from anarchy is never actually crossed, not even in the work of Samuel Beckett, for underlying the tragic vision is the conviction that the meaning of life is to be found in life itself. That is all the literary nihilist can "affirm" in a secular, relativized context. Nature is indifferent like a rock to those potentialities of the spirit which he passionately craves to develop, yet he knows himself to be the one creature whose consciousness, even as it spells out the sentence of his doom, separates him from the realm of instinct and matter.

For the tragic protagonist of the twentieth century there is no miracle of supernatural grace that will make this fatality meaningful. There is no armor against fate. He is punished whether he is innocent or guilty. Even the terms "innocent" and "guilty," like good and evil, are invested with charged overtones of ironic ambiguity. The tragic hero of today is unheroic, in the old sense, because he is by nature a relativist, a creature of paradox for whom all motives are open to question, no passion is pure, no sacrifice justified, no moral victory possible. Though he protests against the absurdity of existence, he makes no effort, in the manner of a Kierkegaard, to transform the absurd into the absolute. He seeks to rise above the myth of the absurd by remaining true to his existential vision of nothingness and by striving to fulfill himself creatively.

iv

Though he focuses his gaze on the specter of the absurd, the modern writer is under no illusion, as we have said, that he has thereby penetrated to the heart of the mystery. Imprisoned in the sphere of history, he learns to accept his finite limitations in a universe which he cannot comprehend. He knows that all human ideals will be defeated and that death is final. Nevertheless, he rebels against the decree of biological fate and refuses to abandon his all-too-human aspirations. That is why, as we have maintained, the tragic vision today has nothing in common with the Christian outlook. Christianity completely reverses the tragic formula: out of failure "success" is born, out of death comes the bliss of everlasting life in eternity. Christianity demands the acceptance of suffering and death as the price of salvation, whereas the tragic vision retains the anguish of uncertainty, the piercing pain of doubt, the dread and fear and despair. If the Christian doctrine is unequivocally affirmed, then it violates the spirit of tragedy, for it insists on a last judgment, a triumph of the divine harmony, the defeat of evil, the redress of unmerited misfortune. Tragedy, as one critic rightly points out, "glorifies human resistance to necessity, religion praises submission." [25]

Even in a secular, relativized universe of values, however, the tragic vision cannot picture life as ruled completely by contingency and unreason or interpret man as the hapless victim of the unresisted blows of evil and the malevolence of fate. Innocence suffering is never justified. The protagonist may fail in his quest for meaning, but even his most agonizing defeat testifies to the greatness of man. The ambiguity of the human condition remains unresolved, but some "affirmation" is made. Maxwell Anderson, for example, setting out to discover the true nature of tragedy, concluded that the essence of the tragic form lies in the spiritual awakening of the hero as he struggles to transcend his animal origins. He is free to choose but his decision must be made without any guarantee that the race of life is worth running, without any assurance even that the collective destiny of mankind has any ultimate meaning. Though in tragedy goodness does not triumph nor is justice vindicated, Maxwell Anderson insists that we must have "a personal, a national, and a racial faith, or we are dry bones in a death valley, waiting for the word that will bring us life. Mere rationalism is death. Mere scientific advance without purpose is an advance toward the waterless mirage and the cosmic scavengers." [26] Maxwell Anderson fails to show us how this idealistic imperative can be incorporated within the dialectic of the tragic vision, which portrays the battle man wages, as he pushes ahead toward the goal of self-transcendence, against nameless, enigmatic powers in a chaotic cosmos that has no concern for his destiny.

This is the central paradox of the tragic vision of our day. The suffering that tragedy enacts makes us face the truth, in all its terror and grandeur, of the human situation and gives us the moral strength to rise reborn out of the grave of despair. Though it makes us behold the most terrifying aspects of existence, its pain and waste and inexpugnable evils, it does not induce a feeling of resignation. Life may be chaos and catastrophe, but the tragic vision protests against the fate of meaninglessness.

Nietzsche had challengingly formulated the nature of the modern tragic struggle: how to live in the face of nothingness. For a philosopher like Heidegger, the essence of tragedy lies in the conflict between illusion and the full disclosure of being. What the tragic vision does in unveiling the alien and the uncanny is to release man from his enslavement to routine; it endows him with the courage to confront the unknown and the prospect of disaster. Abandoning all that he holds dear, the tragic hero is driven to search out the limits of being until he discovers that nothingness is constitutive of the ultimate reality of things. The tragic vision today arises out of the perception that to be human is to stand alone and to suffer gratuitously. The human mind cannot grasp what, if anything, lies beyond. Man searches for a meaning that permanently eludes him. There is no order in the universe that he can recognize as his own. The laws of Nature are not the laws of man. But it is always man who is the hero, man who fights against the beleaguering and ultimately victorious powers of darkness. He fights in order to ensure the triumph of life over death and though in the end he is overcome, he reveals his human greatness in the unequal struggle.

It is out of this attitude of metaphysical rebellion that the tragic vision springs as it highlights the existental dichotomies of the human condition. It is man's awareness that he is different from things-in-themselves, in the Sartrean sense, different from plants and stones, capable of anticipating his own death—it is this awareness that is productive not only of "nausea" but also of the impulse to revolt. Life may be, ultimately, a useless passion, but it is a passion, not a logical conception; an experience lived through, not an abstract idea. The revolt of the modern tragic hero against the oppressive sense of the absurd represents an expression of his freedom to affirm his life. He must arrive at his own decisions, without reference to divinely revealed laws or to a judgment that will be executed in another life. It is the disappearance of the divine promise from the human horizon that has sharppened the paradox of the tragic vision.

We now turn to Kierkegaard in order to analyze the Christian conception of tragedy and show how Kierkegaard's "negative theology" spells the death not only of tragedy but of all art.

KIERKEGAARD must be included among the spiritual precursors of the modern literary revolt; he belongs with such
figures as Schopenhauer, Dostoevski, Nietzsche, Karl
Marx, and Freud. To place Kierkegaard, the spy enlisted
in God's service,[1] in the company of a nihilist like
Nietzsche or a scientific positivist like Freud may seem
outrageously incongruous. The contradiction is easily removed if we remember that Kierkegaard is, like Kafka, an
intrepid explorer of the kingdom of the absurd. What the
modern mind seizes upon avidly is not Kierkegaard's direct religious communications but rather his "aesthetic"
contributions which, composed in a spirit of pseudonymous duplicity and existential irony, reflect his crisis of
fear and trembling before the infinite of nothingness. The
paradox of the absurd can function in one of two ways:
it can give birth to the terrors of nihilism or justify the
dialectics of "the leap." What is so prophetic about
Kierkegaard's pseudonymous, in contradistinction to his
"edifying," work is his amazing insight into the demonism
of doubt. He knew and, like Dostoevski, cogently examined all the reasons that can be advanced in favor of
atheism. He knew that faith must be lived because it is
impossible to prove. Just as Dostoevski is at his best in
setting forth the workings of the mind of the Grand In-
quisitor, which is a reflection of the diabolical in the mind
of Ivan Karamazov, so Kierkegaard faithfully delineated
the etiology of dread and despair.

Though Kierkegaard dealt only incidentally with the theme of tragedy, his "aesthetic" productions have undoubtedly helped to create a climate of opinion that is in keeping with the skeptical temper of our time. It is he who established the category of the absurd and demonstrated the uses of irony and paradox. In the trilogy, *Fear and Trembling, The Concept of Dread,* and *The Sickness unto Death,* he provided a brilliant psychological analysis of the emotions of fear, dread, and despair. Together with Heidegger, he influenced the development of existential analysis in its revolt against the deterministic system fathered by Freud. His pervasive theme is couched in the vocabulary of faith. His writings, nevertheless, pave the way for the emergence of the tragic vision on the modern scene. A philosopher of the Christian faith that is born of the extremity of suffering and despair, Kierkegaard believed that tragedy as a literary form is part of the "aesthetic" stage which must be transcended. He is essentially modern, however, in his exploration of the world within as well as in the furious struggle he waged to reach God. In attempting to demonstrate the emptiness and absurdity of life on earth, the wretched folly of dwelling in the temporal and the relative, he disclosed the tragic plight of human existence when it is not illuminated by the star of faith.

With visionary intensity of insight he grappled with the major problems which plague modern consciousness: the problem of meaninglessness, the limitations of reason, the impossibility of proving the existence of God. It was altogether absurd to believe in God objectively. Therefore, because it was absurd, he believed. Faith is immediacy, subjectivity is truth and truth is subjectivity. It is incomprehensible that God exists and equally incomprehensible that God does not exist. But incomprehensibility is no argument why the positive assumption should not be regarded as valid. The finite mind cannot know God; reason cannot support the burden of faith. As Pascal well knew, God manifests himself to those who seek him out and hides himself from those who do not believe in him.

Kierkegaard is the embattled knight of faith, but his conception of the principle of the absurd has considerable bearing on the aesthetics of the tragic vision. It is a conception, instinct with paradox, that can be used to exalt the faith that is beyond the grasp of reason or to bolster the nihilistic outlook. The myth of the absurd is of such a nature that it can be accepted, as Kafka does, without going beyond it to the affirmation of the divine. Paradox begets paradox and Kierkegaard, far from strengthening the foundations of the faith, as he intended, unwittingly became the prophet of the absurd. An inspired "poet" as well as God-seeker, he was intensely aware of the circularity and infinitude of doubt. Skepticism can go on forever, doubt generating doubt, for once the skeptic holds on to a certainty he ceases to doubt. Faith is therefore a dialectical process. The truth apprehended in inwardness chooses an objective uncertainty with what Kierkegaard calls the passion of the infinite. It is this persistence of the doubt that heightens the drama of the absurd.

Kierkegaard identifies the nefarious principle of the absurd that infects the heart of faith: "The absurd is—that the eternal truth has come into being in time, that God has come into being, has been born, has grown up, and so forth, precisely like any other individual being, quite indistinguishable from other individuals." [2] The absurd inheres precisely in this contradiction, namely, that the Incarnation is the negation of all the categories of human reason. The absurd—and Christianity is the absurd but so is existence—cannot be demonstrated. Like the venture of faith cherished in inwardness, it can only be believed and lived. Christianity, the supreme paradox, is impossible to understand and impossible to believe. The mystery remains an abiding mystery. But if faith transcends the power of human understanding, then there is nothing more to be said. There is no need for art, however tragic the content. The believer believes because it is absurd to believe, and that ends the matter. Kierkegaard courageously faced the challenge of the hidden, inscrutable God, the God who is felt as ultimate reality and yet cannot be known objectively. Since God can not possibly communicate his will to man, the way out of this dilemma is to maintain that God does not communicate directly. The believer who wishes to transcend the absurd must resort to the language of ambiguity and paradox.

Even after the believer makes the leap, the specter of absurdity is not banished. If faith is subjectivity and truth is subjectivity, then it is equally logical to argue that un-faith is subjectivity and that this truth, too, is subjectivity. Why is the passionate subjectivity of a nihilist like Nietzsche less trustworthy than that of the man inspired by faith? If faith creates the object of its belief, unfaith accepts the truth of nothingness. Kierkegaard himself declared: "When an existing individual has not got faith God *is* not, neither does God *exist*, although understood from an eternal point of view God is eternally." [3] Hence it follows that when faith is dead, God ceases to be.

With unsparing honesty of revelation Kierkegaard makes clear the nature of the irreconcilable conflict that attends the absurd quest for faith. In 1850 he makes this entry in his *Journals* under the heading of "The Absurd":

> The 'immediate' believer cannot apprehend the thought that the content of faith is, for the reason and for the third person who is not a believer, the absurd, and that to become a believer everyone must be alone with the absurd. . . . To understand that to the reason it is the absurd, to speak of it thus quite calmly to a third person, admitting that it is the absurd, enduring the burden of the other man looking upon it as the absurd—and nevertheless to believe. While naturally it is a matter of course that for him who believes it is not the absurd.[4]

It is not absurd for the believer because, after he believes, the absurd undergoes a dialectical transformation. Mysteriously transmuted by the agency of faith, it ceases to be absurd. Were faith not an insecure and uncertain possession it would not be faith but a form of knowledge. Only through the category of the absurd can the believer maintain his relationship to God, realizing as he does so that faith proves nothing. The act of belief does not *demonstrate* the existence of God.

Nietzsche hails the death of God and proclaims the

supremacy of the aesthetic view of life. Kierkegaard, whose sole desire is to find God and the secret of eternal life, is not interested in literature or art. He uses writing as a form of prayer. The books he published at his own expense as well as the *Journals* he kept in secret made it possible for him to establish communion with God. His object, as in *Fear and Trembling*, is to defend the basic irrationality of faith. Abraham is the exemplar of the man of faith, prepared to sacrifice everything when God made the call. Here is the knight of faith who, by acting exclusively in the name of God, conquered the temptation of "aesthetics." The authentic believer can, by definition, never become a tragic figure.

The aesthetic life, according to Kierkegaard, is dedicated to pleasure, the consummation of impulse in the instant when it seeks fulfillment. Though the pseudonymous fiction is kept up in *Either/Or*, it is obviously Kierkegaard who orchestrates the various instruments in the counterpointed musical composition. He marshals all his resources of irony and paradox, hyperbole and parable, to show why the aesthete is steeped in sin. Not that the aesthetic life is inherently evil; it is simply neutral. The upshot of the aesthetic stage is despair but not yet absolute despair, the kind that finally leads to a decisive choice of self. The aesthete cannot defeat the implacable enemy, time, that dogs his footsteps and brings all his petty ambitions and endeavors to naught.

Part I of *Either/Or* contains the writings of A, who makes an effort to formulate an aesthetic philosophy, but the putative editor, Victor Eremita, comments: "A single, coherent, aesthetic view of life can scarcely be carried out." [5] In the second volume, B, by contrast, presents an ethical view of life. The point consistently stressed is that A's view of life is "utterly meaningless." [6] A sounds a recurrent note of weariness and futility that is characteristic of the uncommitted aesthetic self. The one who lives aesthetically forfeits his immortal soul and, caught up in the process of dissolution before he is ready to die, sees his life blown away like chaff. Every aesthetic view of life is therefore stricken with despair. Only when one truly despairs does he go beyond despair. By choosing despair, the seeker chooses the absolute, for he is himself the absolute.

Either/Or thus analyzes the existential relation between the aesthetic and the ethical stages as these manifest themselves in existing individuals. The whole meaning of Kierkegaard's message is summed up in the last sentence: "Only the truth which *edifies* is truth *for you*." [7] The ethical man in *Either/Or* embraces despair instead of doubt, but the despair makes it possible for him to choose himself. It is his experience of despair that prepares him for the crisis of inwardness that leads to the religious leap.

In the section called "The Ancient Tragical Motive as Reflected in the Modern," Kierkegaard includes a number of penetrating insights on the tragic genre. Aristotle's prescriptions, he points out, do not exhaust the field of tragedy. The world has changed, man has changed, and consequently tragedy, too, is bound to change. Why must it conform in all respects to Aristotle's "rules"? Kierkegaard recognized that the genius of his age lay in the direction of the comic rather than the tragic. The spiritual bonds that once held the fabric of society together in firm unity have been broken. Deprived of the religious consciousness, the people of his time felt isolated, afflicted with a profound melancholy. Whereas the ancient world was spared the torment of subjectivity, the modern hero, on the contrary, torn up from his communal roots, is interested primarily in his own being. He "stands and falls entirely on his own acts." [8]

Kierkegaard's religious commitment, still discreetly veiled behind a pseudonym, emerges in his belief that evil has no aesthetic interest and that sin is not an aesthetic element.[9] Why is this so? Kierkegaard is combating the secular obsessions of his age, particularly the belief held by many of his contemporaries that every individual is responsible for his own life. If that is the basic assumption, then the downfall of the hero is not in the least tragic; he deserves exactly what he gets. If the energy with which the hero attempts to control his destiny is based on illusion, then the tragic sense is lost. An age that loses the tragic sense falls into despair.[10] The individual hero whom Kierkegaard assailed is a creature of history and time, whose efforts to raise this relativity to the plane of the absolute becomes absolute. Because he must bear the full burden of his guilt, the pain he suffers is all the greater. Alienated from society and the state, thrown completely upon his own resources, he becomes, as it were, his own creator; "his guilt is consequently sin, his pain remorse; but this nullifies tragedy." [11]

In his revelation, particularly in *The Sickness unto Death,* of the numinous, terrifying experience man passes through when he beholds the truth of nothingness, Kierkegaard has much to say that illuminates the conflicts inherent in the tragic vision. Existential dread opens a man's eyes to the deception of which he had been the victim, the lie that he had lived, the emptiness of his existence. Henceforth he restlessly questions the meaning of his life and tries to rid himself of all that makes for inauthenticity or what Sartre calls "bad faith." The experience of dread inspires him with the courage to commit himself absolutely and hazard everything on the outcome. But this drama of inwardness cannot be directly communicated. When the communication is direct it makes little impression, for then the direction is "not inward into the abyss of inwardness, where alone fear and trembling are really fearsome, while if expressed, the fearsomeness remains only if the expression is given a deceptive form." [12] Thus the existential writer approaches the ultimate limit of silence or is compelled to utilize all the resources of indirect communication.

Whereas the second part of *The Sickness unto Death* is devoted to the thesis that despair is sin, and therefore constitutes an "edifying" discourse, the first half analyzes all the difficulties that stand in the way of faith, the varied inducement to rebellion against God.[13] Kierkegaard is seeking to show that despair is not something that befalls one like a disease, but is inherent in man himself. It springs from the paradoxical relationship of man, the finite, to the eternal in him. The sufferer from this sickness unto death cannot endure a life without ultimate meaning. His despair mounts and mounts because he "cannot become nothing." [14] Kierkegaard rightly points out what is central to the character of the tragic vision, namely, that no despair is entirely without defiance.

First comes the despair over earthly felicity, which is a state of pure immediacy. Something external happens which plunges the individual into the gulf of despair. He loses all incentives to action; the foundations of his being have been shaken. He faces the sudden total absence of meaning but fails to perceive that the liberation of the authentic self from despair has nothing to do with the outward blows of circumstance. "Despair over the earthly or over something earthly is really despair about the eternal and over oneself, in so far as it is despair, for this is the formula of all despair." [15] It is also the formula for the despair that overwhelms the modern tragic visionary who has abandoned the promise of the eternal and refuses to humble himself before God.

It is this quarrel with God [16] which signalizes the advent of "the rebel" in modern literature, be he an Ahab or an Ivan Karamazov. Like Dostoevski in *The Possessed*, Kierkegaard fiercely assailed the sacrilegious concept of the God-Man. There can be no shadow of correspondence between God and man. Every doctrine which disregards this qualitative difference "is, humanly speaking, crazy; understood in a godless sense, it is blasphemy." [17] The literature of the tragic vision, in overlooking this difference, is therefore not only blasphemous but "crazy." For Kierkegaard even the effort to achieve salvation through what he calls a poet-existence in the direction of the religious is an expression of sin. Creativity (and this would include all forms of the tragic) is guilty of "the sin of poetizing instead of being." [18]

Kierkegaard's conception of faith has little relevance to the tragic vision. If tragedy befalls a mind that is for the moment agnostic or Manichaean, then it belongs within the Kierkegaardian category of "sin" or "blasphemy." Nevertheless, Kierkegaard's indirect communications have enabled a number of modern writers to gain a deeper insight into the meaning of paradox and the uses of irony in limning the face of the absurd. He taught them, too, to distrust all abstract systems of thought. The existence of a single individual cannot be abstractly formulated; it can only be imaginatively revealed. No individual exists speculatively. The complexities of the human self are beyond the grasp of cognition. Though Kierkegaard's religious intuitions go, as we have seen, far beyond the limits of the tragic vision, he helped a number of writers today by insisting that there was no subject of serious importance but the self. The individual in all his uniqueness becomes the supreme paradox. The self is incommunicable. The attempt to capture the secret of reality is bound to fail.

Kierkegaard was himself a tragic figure in his lifelong obsession with the theme of death. The exceptional man destined to suffer, he faced the terrible alternative: madness or suicide. He opted for "madness," but it was a profoundly creative form of madness. In 1837 he declared that he would give himself to Satan as a means of beholding sin in its most frightful form, a temptation that forms the plot of Bernanos' *Under the Sun of Satan*. Kierkegaard clearly had a taste "for the mystery of sin." [19] But his worst seizures of anguish came from the knowledge that he, like all men, was doomed to die.

He felt, he tells us, like a galley slave, "chained to death; every time life moves the chains rattle and death withers everything—*and that happens every minute*." [20] The thought of suicide continued to obsess him, even though he fought off the temptation. Either suicide is ridiculous (and it is ridiculous if the victim has decided there is actually nothing worth living for) or it is justifiable by reason and then suffering becomes real. But even if suicide offers no solution, the knowledge that it lies within reach, always available, helps to intensify the feeling of life. "The thought of death condenses and concentrates life." [21]

Here is the thanatopsian theme, linked with the metaphysics of suicide, that plays so prominent a role in the literature of the tragic vision. The fact of death determines how life is to be lived, since all of human life is sentenced to death. The "execution," as Kafka shows, may be carried out at any moment, without benefit of a trial. Death, in *Caligula*, is the supreme example of the dreadful contingency of life, and each one must bear this burden alone. Death is not something general or impersonal, a philosophical abstraction, a law of Nature. Kierkegaard wished to know how the conception of death would transform a man's entire life, "when in order to think its uncertainty he has to think it every moment, so as to prepare himself for it." [22] There is a radical difference between thinking about death and actually preparing to die. As Kierkegaard points out, the thought of death becomes a living reality only when the whole life of the existing individual becomes subjectively transformed.

The modern mind is fascinated by Kierkegaard's dialectics of death, his agony of doubt, his paradox of the absurd, even though his struggle for faith sheds only a negative light on the conflicts and complexities of the tragic vision. For him the aesthetic enterprise is a snare and a delusion. The Christian surrenders all desire for self-assertion, particularly that unique individuality which is the source of his creativeness and the ground of his metaphysical revolt. Where God is, tragedy is not.

Most of the modern writers influenced in various ways by Kierkegaard took from him what they could apply to their own condition, and the rest, the deification of the absurd, the "leap" into faith, they rejected.[23] He was their spiritual father, their guide through the underworld of nothingness. He held up for them the image of their alienated self, the terror of time, the contrast between the ephemeral and the eternal, the meaning of despair, the reality of death. He made them aware of the myth of the absurd and the fatality of the human condition. But he wrote aesthetically in order to abolish the need for aesthetics.[24] In the context of his work, faith and the tragic vision are seen to be mutually contradictory terms. The religiously committed man leaps out of time, out of history, out of the sphere of the relative, abjuring all those vain Promethean aspirations that make up the ambiguous testament of the tragic vision.

We must now turn to a more detailed analysis of the nihilistic conditions in the late nineteenth and twentieth century which makes the aesthetics of nothingness the more compelling basis for the release of the tragic vision. Philosophy is not tragedy, though it may, as was true of Nietzsche's writings, set in motion a number of leading ideas and insights which feed the literary imagination of an age. There is the possibility, of course, that both the philosopher and the imaginative writer are reflecting the specific historical circumstances of their *Zeitgeist*. From another point of view, however, both philosophy and literature are expressive of the creative imagination.[25] Nietzsche, like Kierkegaard, certainly belongs to literature. Perhaps Jaspers does too. One is doubtful of Heidegger but there is no question of not including Sartre. All four philosophers—Nietzsche, Karl Jaspers, Heidegger, and Sartre—offer a characteristically modern vision of the tragic.

It is tragic not because it is "pessimistic" or "despairing," but because it spurns all secular solutions. It is Nietzsche in particular who prescribes the conditions that would have to be faced by the literary nihilists of the twentieth century.

3   TWO PHILOSOPHERS OF THE TRAGIC

NIETZSCHE's work offers a fitting introduction to the conflicts and complexities that define the character of the tragic vision. It brings sharply into focus nearly all the major crises of our age of nihilism. This lonely blasphemer against God, who in *Ecce Homo* violently attacked the Crucified, is the prophetic voice of our century. He questioned the belief that sustains all possibilities of faith: the belief in life itself. As Albert Camus points out, Nietzsche, like Heidegger later on, replied in the affirmative to the question of ultimate concern: Can one live, believing in nothing? "Yes, if one creates a system out of the absence of system, if one accepts the final consequences of nihilism." [1] Here is the dialectic of negation at work, the challenging reply to the Kierkegaardian diagnosis of the sickness unto death. It would sweep aside every illusion that blinds man to the naked truth of being. Nietzsche reaffirmed the Kirillovian doctrine that man is entirely alone in the universe, the creator of his own destiny, responsible for everything that takes place.

Schopenhauer's *The World as Will and Idea* was the book that opened the eyes of the young Nietzsche to the truth of existence and launched him on his desperate quest for "salvation." It did away with the conception of God and showed him that the world is inherently evil. Schopenhauer anticipates the nihilistic *Anschauung* of modern literature in his postulation of the thing-in-itself as an expression of the blind biological will, asserting itself with furious but senseless energy. He pictures a universe drained of meaning and purpose. His philosophical Idealism contributed to the aesthetics of meaninglessness.[2]

Nietzsche found inspiration and solace in Schopenhauer's portrait of the creative genius as prophet whose imagination could pierce to the reality behind the phantasmagoric swirl of phenomena and enter the timeless world of deliverance. The artist possessed the saving power of confronting existence in its most enigmatic and terrible aspects. Schopenhauer's work gave Nietzsche a mission: it committed him to "the religion" of Nay-saying. In *The Birth of Tragedy*, his first book, composed under the double influence of Schopenhauer and Wagner, he stressed the unusual capacity the Greeks displayed for depicting life as suffering, their vision of the unmitigated horror of existence, so that their art is designed to make suffering endurable. That is why they sought to transfigure life by portraying it as a fascinating aesthetic spectacle, a thing of beauty existing paradoxically for its own sake, not to be judged in logical or moral terms.

The tragic hero is identified with Dionysus, the god of the myth which discloses that individuation is the primary and perennial source of evil. Tragedy, which both conceals and reveals the heart of Dionysian reality, preserves the illusion that the spectator is witnessing the downfall of one man and not the doom of all mankind. The artist consequently performs an invaluable function in veiling the intolerable truth of nothingness. It is through the mediation of the tragic work of art that the will to live is renewed and redeemed. Nietzsche conceives of God as the eternal artist, constrained by his loneliness to create and then contemplate the pageantry of the phenomenal world.[3] That is why, though art, too, is an illusion, life lives on and art perpetuates itself.

Aesthetic values are the only values Nietzsche at this time recognized as basic. Only by an aesthetic resolution could the nihilistic despair from which modern man suffered so cruelly be overcome. If Nietzsche admired the Greek genius it was because, combining as it did Dionysian excess with Apollonian control, it possessed the sovereign sanity and moral strength to look the Gorgon of horror in the face and still say yes to life. That is the painful decision which the godless man must make: to be rooted in life here on earth, to give up the romantic lie of the Absolute, to be entirely on his own at last.

The Dionysian tragic sense of life is to replace the Christian doctrine of renunciation. Life never perished but went on, without beginning or end. Tragedy is born out of the rites of spring, the riotous rejoicing in the renewal of vegetation, the conquest of death. In the grip of an ineffable ecstasy, the Bacchi released the creative forces slumbering in the depths of the primordial unconscious. It is Apollo, the god of the image, who imposes the necessary restraint on the orgiastic frenzies of Dionysus and his crew. That is how the instinctual power of Dionysus is sublimated and the achievement of the tragic synthesis made possible. It is in this manner that the perception of the absurdity of existence, the *horror vacui*, is transcended, without ever denying the suffering and meaninglessness of life. *The Birth of Tragedy* not only anticipates the mythic interpretation of the tragic form, that was later to be developed more fully by such scholars as Frazer, Gilbert Murray, Jane Harrison, and Francis Fergusson; it prepares the way for the emergence of the tragic vision in the twentieth century.

Written in 1870, *The Birth of Tragedy* explodes the long-held belief that Greek art was fundamentally serene in outlook. If the Greeks arrived at pessimistic conclusions, these were not a sign of decadence but rather an expression of the courage required to bear the worst that life can inflict on man. Why, asks Nietzsche, can not pessimism spring from a plenitude of being so that it represents a release of vitality that felt itself equal to the task of coping with disaster. If the Greek genius turned to tragedy and came to grips with all that was enigmatic and awful in human existence, it did so because of its sheer intoxication with life, its superabundance of energy. What it voiced was a will to tragedy, interpreting all of life, without exception, in aesthetic terms. The aesthetic metaphor exhibited the world as the resolution of God's own internal contradictions, so that the world is the incarnation of a creator who suffers and "for whom illusion is the only possible mode of redemption." [4]

All this sets Nietzsche in opposition to Christianity. Christian thinkers are bound to feel an inveterate antipathy for the conception of art as salvation. Every aesthetic view of life, Kierkegaard held, is infected with despair. Art is a deception to be unmasked, an enticement to be rejected. Nietzsche denounced the Christian mythos as dangerous because it denies life.

> A hatred of the "world," a curse on the affective urges, a fear of beauty and sensuality, a transcendence rigged up to slander mortal existence, a yearning for extinction, cessation of all effort until the great "sabbath of sabbaths"—this whole cluster of distortions, together with the intransigent Christian assertion that nothing counts except moral values, had always struck me as being the most dangerous, most sinister form the will to destruction can take; at all events, as a sign of profound sickness, moroseness, exhaustion, biological etiolation.[5]

The function of the gods in Greek tragedy is to reconcile man to the tragic conditions of existence. It is always life that is affirmed. The lofty symbol of Mount Olympus is simply a fantasy designed to make life bearable. If the Greeks achieved a seeming harmony with the threatening forces of nature, they had to pay a high price for this victory. They could not completely repudiate their relation to the Dionysian spirit; they could not deny the existence of suffering and the frightening aspects of the instinctual world. It is this insistence on the primacy of instinct, the dark powers of the soul, which invests Nietzsche's aesthetics of tragedy with an accent that is authentically modern. Triumphing over subjectivity, tragedy, the highest form of art, projects a haunting vision of the absurdity of existence.

Nietzsche is modern, too, in his contention that the pure tragic consciousness was compromised and corrupted as the cult of rationalism spread in Greece. (In a later chapter we shall try to analyze the effect of the scientific revolution on the structure of the modern tragic vision.) Tragedy, in grappling with the mystery of being, inevitably loses its pristine force of vision if reason gains the ascendancy. If Greek tragedy finally perished, its decline was caused by the triumph of rationalism. After Socrates infected the age, Euripides appeared as the dramatist of the new dispensation. Working faithfully in the Socratic tradition of reasoned analysis, Euripides hastened the death of the Dionysiac spirit.[6] Whereas Aeschylus created, as it were, unconsciously, Euripides mixed his tragedies with rational ingredients. The secret of creativity, Nietzsche insists, is to be found in intuition and instinct, not in reason. Art is opposed to ratiocination. From Socrates stemmed the notion, so fatal to tragedy as well as the tragic vision, that by the power of thought man is capable of fathoming the deepest secrets of being and transforming a contingent universe into a benign and ordered cosmos.

The conflict reduces itself to one between science and art, the rational outlook and the tragic vision. If there is an irreconcilable conflict between the scientific conception and the tragic view of the world, it follows that if tragedy is to be reborn, however changed in form and content, science must acknowledge its inescapable limitations. The struggle to accept and at the same time to qualify, if not reject, many of the conclusions drawn from the scientific system of thought is waged in the work of such writers as Eugene O'Neill, Malraux, Sartre, Arthur Koestler, Albert Camus, D. H. Lawrence, and others. Scientific rationalism avoids dealing with the terrible aspects of reality while the tragic writers refuse to regard the method of reason as the be-all and end-all of existence. It is a gross mistake, Nietzsche argued, to approach myth from the point of view of the analytical intellect. That is how to destroy the freshness and fruitfulness of the mythopoeic imagination. When tragedy disappears, myth dies. The equation is, of course, reversible: with the disappearance of the mythic consciousness, tragedy perishes. Only when it is steeped in myth does a people gain relief from the despotism of reason, the fatality of time, and enter into mystical union with the undying forces of nature.

Nietzsche could not accept the presuppositions of science. The poet and philosopher of nihilism, he was forced to choose between illusion and truth, and he chose, like his literary descendants today, what he felt was the truth, even if it landed him on the other side of despair. Even if he were deprived of the vital beliefs that formerly lent the passion of purpose to his existence, he would not compromise his convictions. A militant atheist, he sought to be rigorously consistent. Truth possessed only subjective validity. He finally arrived at a stage in his intellectual development when he realized that the way to truth lay through the slough of absolute skepticism.

The Joyful Wisdom is an attempt to reconcile this impossible conflict between the will to truth and the realization that the truth is unattainable. The mind perceives the meaninglessness of existence. Such a discovery, however, need not act as a blight on the Dionysian love of life. The metaphysical quest is motivated by a distinctively human passion for order, but it is foolish to humanize Nature, presumptuous to assume that whatever is necessary for the preservation of the human species must actually exist. In *The Dawn of Day*, Nietzsche assails the widespread notion that faith is necessarily a solace and source of joy.

Nietzsche speaks for the modern consciousness when he declares that man must accept what is and cease to delude himself. What lies beyond this earthly existence is unknown. Life is to be affirmed by eliminating the question of God and resolutely confronting all that is fearful in existence. The tragic writer possesses the courage to say "Yea to everything questionable and terrible, he is Dionysian." [7] Only in this way can the tragic spirit transcend the limits of nihilism. In *Thus Spake Zarathustra*, Nietzsche proclaimed his message of "salvation": man must keep faith with his inner being in this life on earth and strive to fulfill all his creative potentialities in a spirit of freedom. He must struggle to surpass himself, even though the universe furnished no pattern of meaning or purpose to which he could dedicate himself. This is the archetypal conflict that runs like a leitmotif through the nihilistic literature of the twentieth century, which bears the unmistakable influence of Nietzschean defiance. By going beyond good and evil, by accepting everything the universe has to offer, by viewing Nature as energy incarnate, perpetually renewing itself, Nietzsche hit upon a way of affirming life as it is. The absurd myth of eternal recurrence, born of the extremity of despair, enabled him to utter his Everlasting Yea. The myth, alas, had little to contribute that could offset the vision of a meaningless universe. It simply drove home the fact that existence was without a goal and paved the way for the Heideggerian apotheosis of Nothingness.

Nietzsche's struggle to rise above the horror of Nothingness provides the central theme of opposition in the modern literature of the tragic vision. It is present, *mutatis mutandis*, in the work of such men as Kafka, Malraux, Sartre, and Camus. Nietzsche sought to restore man to his true estate of freedom. This emphasis on human freedom, this belief that man makes himself just as he invents his gods and shapes the course of history, is part of the metaphysical refrain sounded in Sartre's *Being and Nothingness* and in his plays and novels. Nietzsche could never convince himself that life had a purpose other than the one man arbitrarily assigned to it. Somehow he had to escape the plague of nihilism. As Walter Kaufman says in his study of Nietzsche: "To escape nihilism—which seems involved both in asserting the existence of God and thus robbing *this* world of ultimate significance, and also in denying God and thus robbing *everything* of meaning and value—that is Nietzsche's greatest and most persistent problem." [8] It is also the greatest and most persistent problem of our age.

A skeptic who continued to believe in life, Nietzsche clung to his faith that all art is an affirmation and celebration of life. This provides some ground of creative justification for the metaphysical revolt of the literary nihilists of our time, despite their fixation on time and death and nothingness. Though unable to perceive any sustaining principle of order and justice in the universe, they continue to rebel—and to create. Their symbolic revolt exalts the mystery and grandeur of life. Human existence may be absurd and death the supreme outrage. Nevertheless, long live life! Blessed be the suffering and the madness, the anguish of not knowing, the darkness as well as the light, the final defeat by death even if it is looked upon as a "dirty trick." [9] The writers who behold the tragic vision must bear witness to life as it is.

Nietzsche's tragic pessimism never deviated from its initial aim of celebrating the infinitely creative, if incomprehensible, potentialities of life. Karl Jaspers, who has much in common with Nietzsche, also seeks to escape nihilism and to deal with the difficult problem of tragedy. Whatever the structure of the world may be, man is still under the necessity of living his life and must therefore arrive at a clear understanding of himself. Karl Jaspers' version of tragedy examines the conditions which can make possible the emergence of a new humanism.

ii

Karl Jaspers is under no illusions as to the stupendous difficulties that must be overcome. Man is at present plunged in chaos, seemingly "bound for the void, turning to it in despair or in a triumph of destruction. The cry, 'God is dead,' has been swelling ever since Nietzsche." [10] Modern man is at the mercy of unleashed bestial instincts that in the past were kept within religious or ethical bounds. The only force today that can counter this eruption of violent passions from the depths is the ideal of transcendence, the irrepressible need in man to surpass himself. Like Nietzsche, Jaspers portrays the nature of man as a potentiality that seeks to grow beyond itself. Man is more than the shaped product of heredity, history, and environment. It is his endowment of freedom that makes him specifically human. He is nothing but he is capable of everything. In his finitude he strives to relate himself to the infinite. What seriously retards this quest for transcendence, as Jaspers is well aware, is that the modern cultural community has been badly disrupted.[11]

Beset by a sense of total peril, the consciousness of modern man is best characterized by a series of negations as he faces the future in dire uncertainty. It is not only the extinction of a single civilization that is now at stake but the annihilation of all mankind. But the sentence of doom, Jaspers feels, is not final. Creative humanity must take heart and dare to reach for the seemingly impossible. The ideal of transcendence addresses itself directly to the individual, without mediation. That is how, "God-given to himself," he can become really human. He must follow the truth of his own being, without any guarantee in advance that this is indeed the truth. In short, it is necessary to pass through the desert of nihilism before the soul of man can be liberated for the adventure of authentic being. Hence the paradox: the Nietzschean fall from the absolute "becomes an ability to soar; what seemed an abyss becomes space for freedom; apparent Nothingness is transformed into that from which authentic being speaks to us." [12]

Karl Jaspers analyzes the questions which, in the present as in the past, are basic to the tragic vision. In literature, myth, philosophy, and religion, man asks of the universe: What am I doing here on earth? What am I and what is to become of me? Can I continue to live, believing in nothing? To stop raising these ontological questions is to cease being human. It is these expressions of ultimate concern, ambiguously formulated within an aesthetic context of conflict, that find their way into tragedy. What tragic literature does is to search for the ultimate secret of the world within and the world without. The tragic vision voices the attitude of the hero toward the universe, his response to the fate that is about to overtake him. This is projected not as intellectualized or metaphysical knowledge but as an imaginatively lived apprehension, instinct with dramatic immediacy and intensity of suffer-

ing. The tragic insight the hero gains bears the unmistakable imprint of his age.

As Jaspers rightly points out, the tragic vision varies
through the ages both in form and content. The tragic
consciousness of twentieth-century man is not that of the
Greeks in the fifth century before Christ, when Oedipus
discovered that though he was powerful like a god his
destiny brought him to beggary and blindness. In other
words, in every cultural crisis the enigma of existence must
be interpreted anew. Though Greek tragedy begins with
the affirmation of faith in the will of the gods, it later
begins to question the justice of their actions. In the
Renaissance, Shakespearean tragedy, secular in content,
focuses on the character of man, his overweening ambitions, his pride and potentialities. The twentieth-century
shaper of the tragic vision beholds a universe in which
the gods are dead, since men no longer believe in them.
Necessity is now God, the power of Moira, as impersonal
as it is incomprehensible, to which all must submit.

It is the signal virtue of Jaspers' treatment of the tragic
vision that he perceives the element of continuity which
persists within the ongoing process of change. Tragedy, in
our time as in the past, emerges as man is brought up
short before the truth of his human condition. Peering
into the indifferent heart of existence, he becomes aware
of the war of contradictory forces in his own self. Tragic
knowledge comes into its own when he loses his sense of
being at home on this earth. Early man stoically culti-
vated the ethics of endurance in the face of a dark and
implacable destiny, but this was not yet full-grown tragic
knowledge. In Greek tragedy, however, man questions
existence and his myths are the imaginative embodiment
of his struggle to find out why things are as they are.
He will not be put off by partial or equivocal replies. As
the metaphysical search continues, he becomes progres-
sively more skeptical, beginning to question the justice
and finally the reality of the gods he has himself created.
That is how tragic man at all times strives to adjust himself to a universe that is both enigmatic and threatening.

It is an adjustment, as we shall see, that is inescapably precarious, never grounded in certainty. Tragedy discloses that man does not know himself, the world into which he is thrust, or the destiny to which he has been assigned. He seeks order and discovers only chaos; he reaches out toward the light but remains plunged in nether darkness. Even as he comes to realize that uncertainty is his fated portion in life, he is fearful of sinking into indifference or yielding to the clasp of darkness. His ruling passion is *to know*. Christianity offers him a solution, but it demands that he accept the fate of suffering and the burden of death. Afterwards he will reap his reward in Heaven. Such a theology of redemption is bound to be antitragic. As Jaspers points out, in a Christian framework, every one of man's basic experiences ceases to be tragic. "The chance of being saved destroys the tragic sense of being trapped without chance of escape." [13]

In all tragedy, as Jaspers interprets it, man beholds aspects of existence, nonhuman, alien, and frightening, that have the power to destroy him. But in situations of extreme crisis, his greatness of spirit asserts itself. Though he is a finite part of Nature, subject to its cycles of growth and decay, he also knows that he is superior to Nature in that he can rise above the vicissitudes of time and the visitations of mortality. The tragic hero can never reconcile himself to the operation of blind chance or mindless fate. The tragic vision must somehow disclose the meaning of failure and doom. The doom that lurks in the background and finally pounces upon man is invested with universal meaning, even when all meaning is denied. The tragic vision is the expression of his unconquerable will to truth as he faces the ultimate of annihilation. It liberates the soul of man by imposing some pattern of meaning, however questionable, on the chaotic flux of phenomena. Jaspers, like Nietzsche, reveals the negative conditions in this age of crisis and catastrophe which make it extremely difficult for the motif of affirmation to make itself powerfully felt in modern versions of the tragic vision.

Whereas Greek tragedy depicted the struggle of the

individual against divine powers whose will inscrutably triumphed in the end, the twentieth century witnessed the banishment of the gods from the horizon of human consciousness.[14] They were replaced by Force, Energy, something Wholly Other, the First Cause, that it would be ridiculous to identify as God. Alienated from God, modern man had to fight, as of old, against overwhelming odds and was invariably defeated in battle. Since nothing conquered, he would have to find his vindication in failure.[15] Tragedy reveals the basic cause of his failure, the nature of the reality against which he is pitted, the powers that drive him to the extreme of revolt. By identifying himself with the suffering of the tragic protagonist, the spectator learns that man can stand fast in his integrity even when exposed to the most horrible calamities. The human spirit cannot be broken. It is precisely because man aspires so greatly that his fall is so tragic.

Reality remains ambiguous, life unpredictable, full of terrifying contradictions, but the tragic visionary, in the work of Dostoevski, Melville, Sartre, Faulkner, O'Neill, and Camus, forges resolutely ahead in his quest of the truth. It is this unqualified demand for the truth that makes him heroic. If the knowledge of his own human limitations is at the end forced upon him, he also knows his own strength. Tragedy, according to Jaspers, "shows man as he is transformed at the edge of doom." [16] Jaspers' conception of the tragic thus points the way out of the nihilistic impasse. He warns strongly against the pan-tragic fallacy born of a total lack of faith in life. Wherever such a lack of faith "seeks to parade as a form, it finds the philosophy of nothing-but-tragedy well suited as a camouflage for nothingness." [17] But if every attempt to "deduce tragedy alone as the dominant law of reality" [18] is philosophically unsound, it remains to be seen whether such an attitude cannot be incorporated within the tensions inherent in the tragic vision.

Jaspers is perfectly aware that the tragic destiny of man is acted out in the world of the temporal. The years he spent in Germany under Hitler's rule taught him that history conformed to no universal law. The way things turned out depended on the decisions men themselves make. There is no assurance of divine aid and no possibility of standing still. Each day the battle for values must be fought anew. Jaspers, in replying to his critics, rejects the facile optimism that "is blind to eternity, talks death away, lives as if there were neither dying nor foundering, puts its trust in the intellect; everything will turn out right." [19] True optimism, he contends, peers into the bottomless depths of being and experiences the sense of failure and shipwreck. Jaspers ends *Tragedy Is Not Enough* on a note of humanistic courage. He affirms his vision "of a great and noble life: to endure ambiguity in the movement of truth and to make light shine through it; to stand fast in uncertainty; to prove capable of unlimited love and hope." [20]

Kafka's vision of the absurd is not borne up by this "philosophical faith." It seeks the truth but no light of transcendence shines through it. Kafka's nihilistic universe affords a stark illustration of the tragic vision in the modern age.

4   THE NIHILISTIC UNIVERSE OF KAFKA

> He felt compelled to find some form of affirmation, to affirm something, be it the bare face of existence alone, life simply because and as it is. If Nietzsche was not Kafka's teacher he was certainly his prototype in the desperate attempt to overcome nihilism and discover the secret of new strength of soul, the strength perhaps merely to be, without need of religious meaning.[1]

LIKE Kierkegaard, Nietzsche, and Jaspers, Kafka was profoundly concerned, but as an artist rather than philosopher, with the nature of being, the meaning, always problematical and elusive, of existence. This compulsion to probe more deeply into the heart of reality emerges in his fiction like a neurotic obsession: neurotic because his characters are from the start stricken with an absurd sense of the utter futility of their quest for meaning. Man is forever on trial and finally condemned, the victim of a system of "justice," if it can be called that, which remains incomprehensible. If, according to Kierkegaard, man before God is always in the wrong, the protagonist in Kafka's fictional world is hunted down and caught and disposed of, without reason. The hunger artist, in Kafka's symbolically revealing story, fasted because he could never find the kind of food he liked. Kafka, too, was a hunger artist who never found the kind of food he liked—and spiritually starved to death.

With brooding imaginative insight Kafka labored at the seemingly impossible task of lending form to the modern myth of nothingness. The characters he presents in his novels and short stories suffer chronically from a sense of unreality, unworthiness, and ineffectuality. For it is impossible to deny ultimate meaning without experiencing a corresponding sense of emptiness, a loss of identity. Unlike Renaissance man, inordinately proud of his powers, the Kafkaesque hero has ceased to be self-sufficient. Grimly subjective, he retreats within himself and goes, as it were, underground. He identifies himself with the zoological world. He is consumed with anxiety, running away in dread from an indefinable danger, overcome by despair.[2] If Kafka is such a vital literary figure today, it is because he expressed with such controlled dramatic irony the desperate plight of twentieth-century man, cut off from all sources of transcendence. Seeking in vain to gain the support of a religious faith that reality denied, Kafka shadowed forth a tragic vision that seems to have nothing specifically tragic about it.

Many of his stories center around a character who, himself both accuser and judge, must endure summary punishment without ever understanding the nature of his guilt. Man wanders, lost and alienated, in the night of being, without a fixed destination, but he keeps on wandering, asking himself in perplexity what he shall do to be saved while realizing all the time that there is nothing to be done. Kafka could never make clear to himself the meaning of human existence. Like a sleepwalker he groped his way through the labyrinthine corridors of a dream without end, a dream within a dream, trying to find an answer when he was inwardly convinced no satisfying answer was to be found. As he declares, he wanted to cure his neurasthenia through his creative work, if that could possibly be achieved. Upon reading Kierkegaard he discovered, as he had already suspected, that the two had much in common. "He bears me out like a friend." [3]

What Kafka wanted, above all, was to be freed from his morbid habit of introspection. In "Letter to My Father" he blames himself for his signal lack of character, his miserable incompetence, his inability to face the stern challenge of life. Bowed down with the weight of irremediable doubt, he could not hope to emulate the example set by his strong, dominating father. It is this Oedipus complex which some psychoanalytic critics have pounced upon to explain Kafka's persistent conflicts, both in his life and in his work. Kafka does not fit into this simplified Freudian scheme of interpretation. It fails to account for the unique quality of suffering, his irrational striving, his metaphysical struggles, and his extraordinary gift for transmuting them into works of art.

Enigmatic Jew and artist, a pilgrim exiled from God's kingdom, Kafka was supremely fitted to embody the polarities of the tragic vision: the search for spiritual meaning in a world that exhibited a total absence of meaning. The symbolic motifs that crop up ambiguously in the nocturnal landscape of his fiction have become an *idée fixe* in the literary consciousness of our time. It takes the form of a settled conviction that the human condition is beyond understanding and beyond hope. The writer is of necessity a nihilist who "describes for others the horrors of the world, his own wretchedness and solitude. . . . He established himself in his defeat and converts it into his glory. He proclaims that man is great only by his failures. He wants to fail admirably." [4] This was not penned by Kafka but by a disciple of Sartre, André Gorz, whose book, *The Traitor*, reads like a latter-day version of a Kafka tale, except that it is not fiction but an autobiographical confession. The Existentialist truth that Gorz affirms is one that Kafka would instantly have recognized as his own—"that being has no meaning which is not gratuitous and that every vision of the world is both unjustifiable and true." [5]

This is the mood of spiritual lostness that pervades Kafka's fiction. What makes Kafka an authentic forerunner of the modern tragic vision is that he presents ontological conflicts without ever venturing to suggest a solution; the questions his novels raise cannot be answered; he does not presume to pass judgment on mankind as a whole. Like Kierkegaard, he continues to question God's ways, the problem of suffering and guilt, knowing that nothing is assured, that the finite mind cannot grasp what, if anything, lies beyond. The human condition is beyond redemption. "The metaphysical urge is only the urge toward death." [6] Though Kafka knew that he was doomed to die prematurely from tuberculosis, he never "leaped" to embrace a faith that his skeptical intellect repudiated. He was consistent only in his negations, but the mystery of being continued to haunt him.

Reality for him took the form of a wild processional dance of shadows in the dark of night (it is always night in his world of the imagination), and each of these shadows posed a metaphysical riddle. Even the most insignificant incident took on cosmic overtones of ambiguity. Beneath the humdrum routine of everyday existence, Kafka reveals the irrational conflicts, the anxieties and insecurities, that bedevil the soul of man. He achieves the most fantastic and yet convincing effects of incongruity by dwelling upon homely realistic details so that even the faint intimations of the supernatural seem perfectly credible. "The Burrow" dramatically communicates the meaning of anxiety. We are made to see this animal running wildly here and there, back and forth, widening his cells, building and destroying, and in the process making himself all the more vulnerable. He digs, he broods obsessively on how to protect himself against the invisible enemy, but as he keeps on working and worrying he hears the sound of the beast that will one day destroy him.[7]

Life as Kafka portrays it fails to conform to any rational pattern; it is an expressionistic drama acted out on the stage of a dream in which objects lose their solidity of outline, parallel lines refuse to meet at infinity, two plus two no longer equals four, the laws of logic are violated with impunity, and nothing is certain. Kafka's *dramatis personae* are, like their begetter, trapped in a nightmare of dread from which they cannot break out, and their worst fears, though nameless, finally come true. Reality versus illusion: this provides the internal tensions of the Kafka dialectic. Kafka faithfully depicts the homelessness of man today, the lack of true community—in fact, its impossibility—in a mechanized world that is alien and incomprehensible. The Kafka hero cannot belong anywhere on earth. His consciousness can no longer serve as a test of reality.[8] With disconcerting irony Kafka projects the "why" of existence against the background of the "what," the given, and thus gives birth in his fiction to the category of the absurd. Like Kierkegaard, Kafka could make no sense of the feverish activities of the world of men, their getting and spending, their outbursts of aggression, their collective manias. Truth is beyond the reach of the finite, discursive mind. Subjectivity is incapable of grasping the truth in a relativistic universe.

Yet Kafka the artist knew that the subjective apprehension of the irrational cannot be communicated in irrational terms; if it is not subjected to the disciplined order of art it becomes grotesquely unintelligible, like the euphoric fantasies induced under the influence of mescalin. Like Strindberg in *The Road to Damascus*, Kafka employs expressionistic symbols to represent the madness of the mind, the terrible doubt of appearances, the hellish torment of existence, the nightmare of meaninglessness. He yearns to know the truth, even as he denies that it can ever be attained. His unwillingness to reconcile himself to the dominance of the irrational generates in his work a conflict which, though he is unable to resolve it, makes up the structure of the tragic vision. Kafka's state of metaphysical alienation, as he describes it in his fiction, is the symbolic paradigm of the suffering of all mankind, a parable of the inevitable defeat of the human spirit. The pilgrimage of man is meaningless and yet in some paradoxical way tragic; the tragedy lies in its meaninglessness.

Kafka's work also illustrates the strategic function of irony in the context of the tragic vision. He is not only the artist of the irrational but the skeptic who calls everything into question, including the pervasive element of the irrational. Every fixed point of view, every established value, is turned topsy-turvy. Even the sphere of the commonplace yields glimpses of horror, echoes of the mysterious, ghostly intimations that do not emanate from the natural order, but there is never any assurance that *something* is there. Reality is disintegrated. Chronological time is but an illusion. Facts turn into phantoms. Anything can happen in this universe of the meaningless that is nevertheless governed by an ineluctable fatality. Superseding the laws of logic, Kafka creates an imaginative world that transcends rather than resolves all existential contradictions; it is not tragic because it is absurd, and it is tragic because it is absurd.[9]

In *The Trial*, Joseph K. is summoned to a trial by powers that have no interest in him as an individual. He has, until his thirtieth birthday, led a "normal" life as a head clerk. Then the blow falls. All his secret fears are realized. Gradually the cumbersome machinery of the court, the slow, protracted trial, overwhelms him so that his will is crushed. He can do nothing about his condition. He cannot affirm himself, he lacks the strength to voice his protest against the outrageous absurdity of this "trial." When he is dragged out of the round of inauthentic existence, he is incapable of facing up to a world that is so inscrutable and so hostile. His encounter with the contingent reduces him to a state of trembling impotence; he feels that he is guilty.

Even though he is aware of his guilt, he does not know what he has done which is wrong in God's all-seeing eye. He is never told the reason for his arrest. He has actually done nothing wrong and yet he realizes that he is nonetheless guilty. The novel sums up all the horror of an absurdly irrational universe. The conflict of revolt it sets forth offers no possibility of reconciliation. The hero, no matter what the outcome, will accept nothing less than justice. He will not resign himself to the logic of the Higher Court and he is killed at the end. He cannot believe in God and he finds existence meaningless and intolerable. It is for this reason that he feels worthy of extinction. A challenging version of the tragic vision, *The Trial* introduces a protagonist who, though he serves as a striking example of the anti-hero, the absurd man, is in many ways a lineal descendant of Ivan Karamazov.[10]

Similarly in *The Castle*, the surveyor, Joseph K., cannot discover what his position is to be; his relation to the mysterious Castle remains undefined; he cannot ascertain the will of God. The novel strongly reinforces the pattern of the absurd. The hero frantically tries to reach the Castle where dwell the higher powers that remain aloof and unapproachable. Despite all his setbacks he continues his quest. That is how he asserts his humanity against powers that his reason cannot comprehend. He rejects both the world of the spirit and the finite world of men: the gesture of defiance characteristic of the tragic visionary. He is seeking the ultimate, call it God, but there is no resolution of his conflict. No God, however cruel and contradictory, broods over the Kafka cosmos. The enigma of existence is unresolved.

Some critics have interpreted *The Castle* as the symbolic presentation of a religious quest.[11] One writer insists that Kafka had some intimation of God. "God is the context of his work." [12] Kafka is obviously writing fiction, not propounding theological conundrums, but *The Castle* lends little support to a purely religious interpretation. K. is not an allegorical character. He receives ambiguous messages from the Castle but the text vouchsafes no explanatory clues. The action neither affirms nor denies the faith.

K.'s single purpose is to find the truth if he can. The Castle may hold the answer he craves, but he is uncertain on this score. What troubles him, as it did the author, was the problem of justifying his existence.[13] Though he felt sure of his mission when he first arrived in the village, his experiences gradually undermine his confidence. He becomes skeptical; things are not what they seem. He feels completely helpless. His struggle to achieve certainty is frustrated by his growing awareness of the hopelessness of his quest. If at the end he resigns himself to the mystery beyond understanding, that is by no means to be construed as the visitation of grace. Those who place a theological gloss on *The Castle* are going beyond the confines of the work itself.[14] The curtain of doubt is never lifted. Kafka's characters eternally debate the question of existence, but their struggles and suffering yield no conclusions. Man must dwell forever in uncertainty, but he never ceases to question. Kafka is himself the hapless victim he describes in his fiction, never resigned to the mystery that defies the light of human understanding. Art is his prayer but it is also his perdition. There is no strictly religious element in his novels and short stories, no reflection of the divine, only an intimation of the absurd that is beyond all reason.

This poses a difficult problem. Kafka, though dwelling in a godless world, continued to regard himself as a "religious" man. His literary career is the record of this paradoxical struggle. The meaning of Kafka's entire work, according to Gunther Anders, "is governed by his awareness of the 'death of God.' "[15] The absence of God provided him with the incentive to seek for God. If he sought some means of salvation, however, it was not because he was religious in his orientation, "but because he felt compelled to find some form of affirmation, to affirm something, be it the bare fact of existence alone, life simply and because it is. If Nietzsche was not Kafka's teacher he was certainly his prototype in the desperate attempt to overcome nihilism and discover the secret of new strength of soul, the strength perhaps merely to *be*, without need of religious meaning."[16]

That is the negative metaphysical obsession from which Kafka suffered. Some critics have denounced him for his dark pessimism, his presumption in elevating his private manias into a credo of absolute negation. J. P. Hoodin rightly feels behind Kafka's metaphysical fear "the revenge of the despairing, the rebellious, driving right into the midst of the Absolute, against the logic of creation, against a performance in which man seems to be nothing but a bad joke on the part of Providence."[17] What of that? What is here castigated as an insufferable weakness is actually the formula of the tragic vision, the principal source of Kafka's strength, the creative qualities that enabled him to explore and give expression to the dread and despair of the human condition. Nonreligious in his insights, he shows that all striving is futile. Neither his life nor his work can be subsumed, without casuistic stretching, under the category of the holy. The man who could say, "We are nihilistic thoughts that came into God's head," [18] could not be at home in any tabernacle of faith.

All his life long he remained the doubter, even if it plunged him into absolute darkness. His characters strive to reach the truth but they are never capable of mobilizing the energy required for a genuine act of defiance. They are guilty and they know they are doomed. They accept their punishment and do so without the satanic questioning of an Ahab or an Ivan Karamazov.[19] Kafka foreshadows the literary Existentialists of our time in suggesting that the metaphysical quest fails to get anywhere. He differs from them in that he cannot get himself to believe that life is its own justification or that revolt is any less absurd than resignation to the myth of the absurd. Though his characters lack the courage to rebel in the name of the absurd, they cannot throw off the burden of the mystery and take refuge in the inauthentic life. The problem they face is the problem the genius of Nietzsche had divined: how affirm life in the face of nothingness.

It is the vision of the absurd which must be transcended by an act of revolt if it is to be transformed into the tragic vision. This is the difficult task to which Albert Camus addressed himself in his philosophical and creative work.

ALBERT CAMUS AND THE
    REVOLT AGAINST THE ABSURD

> I continue to believe that this world has no ultimate
> meaning. But I know that something in it has meaning and
> that is man, because he is the only creature to insist on
> having one. This world has at least the truth of man, and
> our task is to provide its justification against fate itself.
> And it has no justification but man; hence he must be
> saved if we want to save the idea we have of life.[1]

THE PASSAGE THROUGH the dark night of the myth of the
absurd leads either to the absurdity of faith or the absurdity of nothingness: the God of Kierkegaard or the defiant nihilism of Nietzsche. The first is embraced with
passion only by the sacrifice of reason, so that a new tran-
scendental truth of the spirit emerges, not circumscribed
by the categories of earth-bound logic. The writer who refuses to relinquish the power, however finite and fallible,
of reason must root himself in the life of this earth and
accept the demonic consequences of the challenge of the
absurd; he must bear the full responsibility for his destiny
in a universe which offers no justification whatsoever for
his aspirations or his ethical commitments.

The subjective conviction that life is essentially meaningless—it is one metaphysical perspective among many
that are available to the writer—must be concretely embodied within the formal unity of the work of art. Kafka
showed how difficult a problem this posed for the creative
imagination. The tragic vision is indispensable in that it
seeks somehow to reconcile man to his absurd fate, a

reconciliation that must take cognizance of the hopeless conflict between the cosmic and the human. It must face courageously the knowledge of the inevitability of death. But when God is totally absent in the world of man, the writer is at a loss how to work out a metaphysical resolution. The distinctively modern form of the tragic vision no longer concerns itself with the fall of the House of Atreus, the vindication of a universal principle of divine justice. Modern tragedy, Camus asserts, will no longer busy itself with the adaptation of Greek myths.[2] He is certain that "a great modern form of the tragic must and will be born . . . certainly I shall not achieve this; perhaps none of our contemporaries will. . . . But this does not lessen our duty to assist in the work of clearance which is now necessary so as to prepare the ground for it." [3]

The tragic vision must and will be born! Underlying this categorical imperative is the assumption that the modern writer must do everything in his power to prepare the way for its birth. Unfortunately the way is beset with pitfalls and perils. It is not enough for the writer to reveal the worst that can befall man. If that is all he communicates, he still falls short of the authentically tragic vision. No, if the tragedy he composes is to sound the note of affirmation, he must unfold some meaningful correlation between freedom and necessity, between the choices the hero makes in a contingent universe and the fate that finally overwhelms him. Otherwise the protagonist is the mere sport of chance, a victim of the fortuitous, like the inhabitants at the foot of Mount Vesuvius who are one day suddenly destroyed by a violent eruption of lava. Whatever the metaphysical foundation on which it rests, the tragic experience must affirm life and celebrate, as we have said, the greatness of the human spirit.

From the time of Nietzsche to the present, this is the plight of the writer who endeavors to erect the structure of the tragic vision on a nihilistic base. If life is indeed a thing of sound and fury, if in the end there is no difference between the loftiest strivings of the spirit and the gratification of animal instinct, then the attempt to create tragedy would seem to be foredoomed to failure. And yet, throughout the history of the race, tragedy has been a universal mode of expression. Without it the people perish, succumbing to *tedium vitae*, losing their love of life. The myth of the absurd, the nightmare of contingency that Kafka and the literary Existentialists of our day regard as the ruling principle of the universe, incapacitates man for that creative release of Dionysian energy, that ecstatic affirmation of life, which the tragic vision paradoxically calls forth. If the writer is of the belief that art, too, is a meaningless endeavor, then there is no reason why he should take the trouble to persist in his mission. The postulation of the metaphysics of the absurd raises a contradiction which, if not overcome, threatens to plunge art into anarchy.

Camus's own career cogently demonstrates that the only way in which the tragic vision can rise into being is by defying the absurd. Camus does not repudiate the truth of the absurd; he simply goes beyond it. Like Sartre, he knows there are no eternal verities, no table of commandments brought down from Mount Sinai. Man is alone and therefore responsible for choosing his own values in a spirit of freedom. The tragic vision is born when nihilism is transcended by an ethic of human responsibility. Even during the terrible years of crisis when the Nazi armies conquered Europe, Camus never yielded to despair but continued to proclaim the ideal of justice.[4] The world is absurd but not the destiny man chooses for himself or the ideals he struggles to establish on earth. Fate becomes destiny, and the modern tragic visionary, like the hero of *The Plague*, steps forth on the literary scene.[5]

This victory over the aesthetics of the absurd was not easily gained. Camus's creative strength derives not from his ideational faculty but from his capacity for responding sensuously to the variegated beauty of the earth. Like the Algerian people among whom he was born, he appreciates "The glories of our blood and state" as substantial things, not shadows, and therefore looks upon death as the enemy. It is the intrusion of death that transforms the Garden of Eden into a charnel-house of horror, so that the human quest for happiness turns into a curse. The precarious present is all a man can hope to enjoy. Hence the necessity for revolt. The crime of crimes is to resign the self to this intolerable condition, to sink into the morass of routine, even if it is done in the name of duty. There is the dichotomy which is a perpetual source of anguish in man: the craving for life without end is opposed by the knowledge that he is doomed to die. Camus, like Heidegger, feels that it is death which casts a ubiquitous shadow of dread over all of life. Alienated from Nature, enslaved to death, the hero in Camus's early work assumes a destiny that is metaphysically absurd.

The transcendence of the absurd, without rejecting those features of nihilism that make human freedom possible, was, in Camus's case, not achieved without an intense struggle. He had to discover some principle of justification for life. In the beginning he had to work with a nihilism that undermined the very basis of human existence. When he heard of the mass murders the Nazis had carried out and the tortures they inflicted on the fighters in the Resistance movement (he was one of them), he fell for a time into a mood of absolute despair, but he overcame it. Even if it were true that life on this planet had no meaning beyond itself, he believed that man at least makes sense. "This world has at least the truth of man, and our task is to provide its justication against fate itself. And it has no justification but man; hence he must be saved if we want to save the idea we have of life."[6] After his initial exploration of the myth of Sisyphus, he composed The Plague and The Rebel, both of which voice his message of rebellion.

It is fascinating to watch Camus's dialectical struggle to escape from the closed universe of the absurd of Kafka and Heidegger. The human being irrationally expects the world into which he is born to be governed not only rationally but justly, but if existence is entirely without reason then it is foolish to look for a sustaining pattern of justice. Life can neither be explained nor justified. Reality is forever enigmatic, utterly unknowable. Though reason is impotent to penetrate the mystery of being, yet without its support man is rendered completely helpless. From the defeat of reason, Camus drew the conclusion that all absolutes must be scrapped. All truths are human truths, and therefore relative to the man who believes in them. The category of the absurd is not a logical product, even though it is confirmed by the intellect.

Camus' early work tried to utilize the myth of the absurd and invest it "with much of the intensity, inevitability and universality of classical tragedy." [7] Death, as in *Caligula*, is the crowning feature of the absurd. Just as all truth must be uncompromisingly faced, so must one learn to live with the absurd, not by resigning himself to it but by revolting against it. The absurd is thus transformed into a kind of "negative" religion, providing the spiritual basis on which the tragic affirmation can stand. The absurd, like "nausea," confronts the ineffable strangeness of reality, the plethora of alien things in Nature that have no relation to the self. But the contradictions inherent in such a vision are never resolved. Although the universe altogether fails to conform to the demands of logic, the human longing for order cannot be cast aside as a sorry illusion. For Camus as well as Sartre the old standard formulas had failed completely,[8] and they engaged in a brave creative struggle to invent a tragic "formula" of their own.

In *The Myth of Sisyphus*, Camus drew a lucid picture of the absurd man of the twentieth century, the man who has traveled beyond the last outpost of reason and gazed into the heart of darkness. Henceforth he must dwell in a universe that is inexplicable, but he cannot overcome the feeling of dread that overtakes him as he faces the absurdity of existence in a world in which nothing lasts. Life fails to make sense. The tragedy of man lies in his realization that this is so. But if the absurd has meaning, then it is "only in so far as it is not agreed to." [9] Like Meursault in prison waiting to die, the absurd man ceases to believe in the future and surrenders all hope. Camus denies flatly that the experience of the absurd leads to God. One must cling to the truth even if it does not satisfy the Pascalian "reasons" of the heart. These are the formidable contradictions that plagued Camus as he labored to produce a tragic art that is dedicated to the revelation of the absurd.

The virtue of the myth of Sisyphus is that it compels man to recognize the hopelessness of his situation. Meursault, in *The Stranger*, is the absurd hero who has gained the insight that nothing matters. Having cast off the moral illusions to which society and his judges pay sanctimonious lip-service, he is concerned solely with the sensation of being alive. While in prison he begins to think like a "free" man and yet he grows accustomed to the prison routine. One can get used to anything. He is stricken with no sense of guilt for shooting the Arab. Who can tell where the path of his life may lead? "I've always been far too absorbed in the present moment, or the immediate future, to think back." [10]

Now he stands condemned to die, but then each man is doomed by this evil necessity. Death is a foregone conclusion and one must submit. What difference does it make, he asks himself, whether one dies at thirty or seventy? In the end one must die just the same. All he wants after death is to remember this life on earth. Though he was sentenced to die, he was sure of his present life and sure of his coming death. This was the only certainty he could count on.

> I'd been right, I was still right, I was always right. I'd passed my life in a certain way, and I might have passed it in a different way, if I'd felt like it. I'd acted thus, and I hadn't acted otherwise; I hadn't done x, whereas I had done y or z. And what did that mean? That, all the time, I'd been waiting for this present moment, for that dawn, tomorrow's or another day's, which was to justify me. Nothing, nothing had the least importance, and I knew quite well why. . . . From the dark horizon of my future

a sort of slow, persistent breeze had been blowing toward me, all my life long, from the years that were to come. And on its way the breeze had leveled out all the ideas that the people had tried to foist on me in the equally unreal years I then was living through. What difference could they make to me, the deaths of others, or a mother's love, or his God; or the way a man decides to live, the fate he thinks he chooses, since one and the same fate was bound to "choose" not only me but thousands of millions of privileged people who, like him, called themselves my brethren. . . . Every man alive was privileged; there was only one class of men, the privileged class. All alike would be condemned to die one day; his turn, too, would come like the others'.[11]

In this Heideggerian passage of reflection, Meursault tries to comprehend the meaning of the past, to trace a pattern of causation in the vicissitudes of his life that had brought him to this absurd climax of fate. Though he embraces a philosophy of supreme indifference, he does, by implication, strike a note of defiance. His ability to face death courageously represents a kind of freedom achieved. Meursault, the personification of the absurd, is Everyman. There is nothing "tragic" in the murder he commits or the consequences it brings about. It is his armored indifference that cuts him off from the tragic vision. He fails to fight against the tyranny of the absurd, but his passiveness is in itself a form of revolt. His final insight raises him above the deceptions of inauthentic existence. The truth must be disclosed. It is cowardly as well as futile to hide from this final disclosure of the total indifference of a mechanical and therefore absurd universe. In such a universe, the concept of guilt is wholly irrelevant. It is this consciousness of the inescapable absurdity of existence that prevents Meursault from acquiring the noble stature of a tragic hero.

Camus is not formulating a thesis. He is writing a novel, even though he is aware that art has no ultimate importance. Sartre calls *The Stranger* a leaf taken from Camus's life. "And since the most absurd life is that which is most sterile, his novel aims at being magnificently sterile. Art is an act of unnecessary generosity."[12] No tragic art is sterile. No writer can produce the tragic vision if he is seriously committed to the proposition that life is essentially absurd. The literature of the tragic vision must do more than record the hero's inglorious struggle against the implacable absurdity of death; it must also reveal his capacity for revolt. Before turning to the aesthetics of revolt, we must consider briefly Camus's contribution as a playwright of the absurd.

ii

From the beginning Camus sought to create a form of tragedy in which man would be presented as the doomed victim. His early plays marked an attempt, earnest though unsuccessful, to shape tragedy out of the knowledge that life is meaningless. *The Misunderstanding* is, like *The Stranger*, a representation of the encounter with the absurd. It is not tragic in structure or content simply because the absurd is not tragic.

Influenced in his conception of tragedy by the writings of Nietzsche, Camus held that tragedy emerges when two equally strong forces are in conflict. Man must assert his desire for freedom, but he meets the resistance of an external order that is indifferent to his needs, and these conflicting forces cannot possibly be reconciled. The Camus protagonist is, like Kafka's heroes, a victim; the fate meted out to him is one that his mind cannot grasp. In his battle against death, however, he beholds the blinding truth which redeems him from the clutch of illusion. *The Misunderstanding*, written in 1943, reiterates the theme that the human condition is hopeless. There is no possibility of divine help. The only peace open to the deprived human being is to take on the indifference of stone, the immobility of death. There are no answers to man's questions.

In *Caligula*, Camus presents the absurd hero *in extremis*, the protagonist who has shed all the beliefs that men cherish in order to make life bearable. There is no truth, and art is only a species of make-believe. Caligula is made mad by his discovery that at the heart of the uni-

verse there is only nothingness; hence all striving is useless. The world is without meaning. Whereas *The Misunderstanding* culminates in a double suicide, *Caligula*
introduces a hero who indulges in murder. After losing
Drusilla, the sister whom he loves, the Emperor cannot
accept things as they are. He will kill off his subjects
wholesale and teach them the bitter lesson of death. In
severing his bond with mankind, he engineers his own
destruction. As Camus declares:

> One cannot destroy everything without destroying oneself.
> That is why Caligula depopulates the world around him
> and, faithful to his logic, does what is necessary to arm
> against him those who will eventually kill him. *Caligula* is
> the story of a superior suicide. It is the story of the most
> human and most tragic of errors. Unfaithful to mankind
> through fidelity to himself, Caligula accepts death because
> he has understood that no one can save himself all alone
> and that one cannot be free at the expense of others.[13]

Though Dostoevski would have been attracted by such
a theme, he would have rejected the nihilistic logic of the
absurd. Camus, however, is fascinated by the character of
the absurdist hero who rebels in vain. With imaginative
passion Camus develops the theme that because men die
they are stricken with absolute despair. Caligula is resolved to open the eyes of men to the truth about this
world—"which is that it has none." [14] When he is accused of blasphemy, he replies: "Blasphemy? What's
that?" [15] Like Meursault, he has come to feel that nothing
matters. At the end he arrives at the understanding that
wholesale murder is not the solution. But who, he asks,
can condemn him "in this world where there is no judge,
where nobody is innocent?" [16]

The test of "the sincerity" of the literary nihilists in
France came during the Second World War when Hitler's armies turned their country into a prison. Camus,
like Sartre, took an active part in the underground movement. In "Letters to a German Friend," published in
1943 and 1944, he confessed his belief that the world was
devoid of ultimate meaning, and he still thought so, for

it was true. But if God does not exist, it does not follow that the end justifies the means or that might is the final arbiter of history. To believe that nothing matters, that man is contemptible, to be killed off as the occasion demands, to make power the touchstone of morality—that is the madness of nihilistic despair. The plague of totalitarianism had to be combated, the myth of the absurd had to be transcended. If life is incomprehensible, then it behooves man to bring meaning into the world and thus affirm his birthright of human freedom. Camus raised aloft the banner of metaphysical revolt. Art is a protest in the name of life against the immutable decree of death. That is how Camus sought to affirm life and repudiate the nihilism on which his vision of the absurd is based.

iii

Camus was far from happy in his role as artist of the absurd. Not that he ever succumbed entirely to its spell. His treatment of the theme invariably contained an implicit element of defiance. In venturing to ask whether man can choose his own values without relying on the supernatural, Camus was already stepping outside the limits of the absurd. The refusal to acquiesce in the fact of death compels man to face the meaning of his existence. He will accomplish nothing by his revolt except an intensification of the sense of being alive. Abandoning as hopeless the romantic quest for the absolute, the metaphysical rebel leaves behind him the burden of the absurd. He does what he can to relieve human suffering, without seeking a higher principle of justification. That is the "positive" faith which animates Dr. Rieux in *The Plague*.

Camus in this novel raises the same question that harrowed the conscience of Ivan Karamazov: why must the innocent be made to suffer? The name of God can no longer be invoked to justify the cruel contradictions and suffering of existence. Man must rely on his own powers as he struggles to fashion a world which will be meaning-

ful because it is human. He must take upon himself responsibility for creating values in an absurd universe. If
redemption is to be postponed until Judgment Day, then
the injustices that infest the earth will be allowed to go
on until the end of time. Like Simone Weil, Camus insists that all, without exception, must be saved. The absurdist hero is thus transformed into a metaphysical rebel
who dedicates himself to life not death, to affirmation not
denial. Camus sums up the formula of conflict that informs the tragic vision of our time:

> I proclaim that I believe in nothing and that everything
> is absurd, but I cannot doubt the validity of my own
> proclamation and I am compelled to believe, at least, in
> my own protest. The first, and only datum, that is furnished
> me, within absurdist experience, is rebellion. Stripped of all
> knowledge, driven to commit murder or to consent to it,
> I possess this single datum which gains great strength from
> the anguish that I suffer. Rebellion arises from the spec-
> tacle of the irrational coupled with an unjust and incom-
> prehensible condition. But its blind impetus clamors for
> order in the midst of chaos, and for unity in the heart of
> the ephemeral.[17]

The spectacle of the irrational coupled with an unjust
and incomprehensible universe, the blind impetus that
clamors for order in the mist of chaos: this serves to identify the battle of forces that is fought out within the
framework of the modern tragic vision. If to rebel is to
exist, then it is the duty of the rebel to fight against the
absurd destiny of meaninglessness. *The Plague* is a passionate protest directed not only against death but also
the suffering and injustices imposed on mankind. Dr.
Rieux, the hero as rebel, embodies the ethics of defiance.
He can not get used to seeing people die in the plague-
stricken Algerian city. That is why he speculates: "Since
the order of the world is shaped by death, mightn't it be
better for God if we refuse to believe in Him and struggle
with all our might against death, without raising our eyes
towards the heaven where He sits in silence." [18] This is a
far cry from the hysteria of a Caligula or the passivity of

a Meursault. Bound to humanity by the solidarity of suffering, the rebel fights against the plague, sustained solely by the power of compassion. It is the story of human revolt, not the myth of the Fall, that Camus bodies forth in *The Plague*. Dr. Rieux speaks in the name of man, not God. The truth must be served. Humanity must adjust itself to things as they are. The essential nobility of man emerges in his revolt against the fate of death.

In *The Fall*, Camus emphasizes the need to cultivate a sense of human limitations. No man is God. Nature may be indifferent to the upsurge of human aspirations, but man must labors steadfastly at building the city of Jerusalem. In *The Fall*, Camus analyzes the condition of spiritual emptiness and desolation which overwhelms those who live for pleasure alone; they can no longer hide from themselves the nothingness toward which they are borne by the onflowing currents of the river of time. The novel exhibits the struggle in the heart of man between egotism and altruism, instinct and conscience. No one is innocent. Camus is striving to discover on what terms existence can be justified, but he is still unreconciled to a world in which man is doomed to die.

Camus died before he could fully develop his concept of tragedy. The myth of the absurd failed to give birth to the tragic hero. The literature of revolt did introduce characters who aligned themselves with suffering mankind. Since there is no world beyond, man must, as Camus contends, make his finite experience an end in itself. Life and death are two poles of a single, ongoing process. Conflict is of the essense of life, darkness and light, uncertainty rather than absolute knowledge, pain and frustration and defeat as well as pleasure and fulfillment and triumph. It is this acceptance of the necessity for the struggle, even though it falls invariably short of the goal, that can lend exhilaration to the tragic experience. This experience can best be exemplified by a hero who is possessed of greatness of soul.

Unfortunately the potentialities for affirmation present in the literature of revolt were overshadowed by the myth of meaninglessness which lay like a blight upon the cultural landscape. A universe drained of ultimate meaning drove home the lesson of the insignificance of man. It raised the haunting question of why continue to live if all that man has thought and aspired to reach comes in the end to naught. As Edwin Arlington Robinson says:

> *'Twere sure but weaklings' vain distress*
> *To suffer dungeons where so many doors*
> *Will open on the cold eternal shores*
> *That look sheer down*
> *To the dark tideless floods of Nothingness*
> *Where all who know may drown.*

Camus went as far as he could go, before his life was cut short, in laying the foundations of the tragic vision.

BEFORE CONCLUDING this section on nihilism and tragedy, we shall examine the character of the tragic hero in our time and what distinguishes him from the tragic hero of the past. All tragic literature, from the time of the Greeks to the present, makes assertions of some kind, however equivocal, about the nature of man. These assertions emerge ambiguously, never explicitly, from the context of the work of art. Sophocles, Aeschylus, Euripides, Dante, Shakespeare, Marlowe, Cervantes, Melville, Eugene O'Neill, Tennessee Williams, Kafka, Camus, Céline, Robinson Jeffers, Sartre, Samuel Beckett, each of them is holding up a many-sided mirror to the ever-changing spiritual face of man. In general, the tragic vision has tended to interpret man from two sharply opposed points of view. In the one he is represented as made in the image of God, instinct with greatness. In the other, he is represented as being, like plants and animals and instinct, a part of Nature. In Shakespeare's plays, human life, despite the indifference of the gods, is charged with the power of greatness. Hamlet wonderingly declares: "What a piece of work is a man! how noble in reason! how infinite in faculty! in form and moving how express and admirable! in action how like an angel! in apprehension how like a god! the beauty of the world! the paragon of animals!" [1] Or the hero may be portrayed in the light of both or many perspectives fused. Saints and nihilists, each of whom is justified in his own right, appear in the universe of Dostoevski's fiction: Ivan and Smerdyakov and Alyosha, Myshkin and Rogozhin. Nietzsche calls man a beast of prey, but Oswald Spengler questions whether this is an insult to man or beast.[2]

In *The Modern Temper*, Joseph Wood Krutch laments the loss of the heroic world of the past. Our tragedies are pallid compared to those of the Greeks and Elizabethans. Modern drama and fiction concern themselves principally with the distresses of petty and constricted souls. What Krutch stresses is that tragedy cannot be separated from the idea of nobility. What is wrong with our age is that it has lost its faith in the greatness or the capacity for greatness of man. Hence it is incapable of rising to the heights of the tragic vision. The modern mind is incapable of creating the hero who will bear the passion and splendor of the tragic conflict.

Our discussion thus far has shown that the tragic vision today does not concern itself with exceptional individuals, endowed with the power of self-affirmation. Alienated from Nature and God, bowed down by his own spiritual impotence, modern man has shrunk ignobly in stature. A conditioned creature of his *Zeitgeist*, he is consumed by a feeling of purposelessness, believing in nothing. Besieged by doubt, divided within, he is engaged in a perpetual monologue of introspection. The Kafka hero confronts a mysterious world which vouchsafes no reply to the questions he raises in his dire perplexity. He cannot assert himself, for he has no self to affirm. What for Sartre flashes up before consciousness in a moment of "nausea," the vision of an alien and contingent universe of things, is for the Kafka hero a permanent and inescapable condition. Having thrown off all illusions, or so he thinks, Camus's absurdist hero faces the universe without any lofty faith to sustain him. Imprisoned in his subjectivity, the Existentialist hero in Sartre's work constitutes his own metaphysical problem. Dying is as meaningless and absurd as the passion of living.

The Greek tragic writers affirmed the indomitable greatness of the human spirit. They knew that everything has to be paid for; no transgression went unpunished.

The crimes of the House of Atreus must be avenged and the Erinyes arrive to act as the agents of the gods. The *Choephori* makes it clear that those who are guilty of shedding blood must have their own blood spilled. The gods work invisibly behind the scenes to uphold the Law, so that the order of the universe will not be overthrown. On the modern scene, however, no pattern of justice triumphs. Nihilism is in the saddle. The sense of doom has seized man by the throat and is slowly choking the will to live and the love of life out of him.

The moral and spiritual safeguards, which mankind had so painfully fought to establish through the ages, were wiped out in the holocaust of the Second World War. The furies of horror were unleashed, not only the experiment in atomic annihilation but the spectacle of genocidal infamies perpetrated upon millions of innocent people. Gottfried Benn was right: the Lutherian screams of protest in a Faustian skirmish were silenced. Totalitarianism rode rough shod over all the values of life. The inmates of the concentration camps were transformed into beasts or corpses. One of the survivors tries, in retrospect, to invest his experience with meaning. The suffering, however terrible, which life entails must be accepted. Even death, Viktor E. Frankl concludes in *From Death-Camp to Existentialism*, can be made meaningful if man strives with responsible freedom to fulfill the potentialities of the present. That is the only way of combating the plague of nihilism, a philosophy which says "that being has no meaning; a nihilist is a man who considers being (and above all, his own existence) meaningless." [3] But most of the prisoners in Nazi concentration camps were too close to the reality of death to raise ultimate questions.[4] As history turned efficiently cruel and nihilism shattered the image of the unity of mankind, the private self was liquidated. This crisis of selfhood became one of the central and obsessive themes of the tragic vision.

ii

Science, by deliberately excluding the element of the subjective in its calculations, the human variable which cannot be empirically measured, forced man within a mechanical system of causal necessity. In the deterministic universe that science postulates there is no room for the play of desire, ideals, or teleological concepts. The scientific outlook is neither tragic nor antitragic; it is fundamentally untragic. It proceeds with its inquiries *as if* man were a machine, a physico-chemical organism. How disconcerting to human pride to discover that man, "in apprehension like a god," is, after all, but a machine, a configuration of molecules of organic matter ephemerally inhabiting the earth.

The conception of man as a machine—that could not be the final truth about human nature. It was a conception that could not be fitted within the framework of the tragic vision. (This problem will come up for further discussion in the next section dealing with the relation of science, psychoanalysis, and Marxism to tragedy.) The modern mind is bombarded by a host of competing ideologies, conflicting interpretations of the self. According to Erich Fromm, man, the sole measure of value, strives to fulfill himself, to live in the light of those moral concepts he has himself chosen. He is therefore not the product of his environment or a function of the socio-economic order. Fromm's humanistic philosophy, which resembles Sartre's Existentialism in a number of respects, regards man as a part of Nature and yet homeless on earth. The dichotomies which are rooted in the condition of human existence cannot be overcome.

Existential analysis, which derives some of its leading insights from the work of Kierkegaard and Heidegger, sought to revise radically the concept of "homo psychologicus" by showing that each human being, unlike the animal with its built-in apparatus of instincts, is endowed with manifold potentialities of becoming. He is not a machine. Though he dwells in a physical universe of matter and mass and energy, he does not behave like an electron. He knows himself, he is responsible for making himself, he faces the prospect of his own death. Indeed, existential analysis, like the literary Existentialists, sees man as always caught in a state of becoming and therefore perpetually in crisis. This is the crisis of selfhood that is reflected in a large body of modern literature. It is the widespread acceptance of the scientific conception of man as a machine that accounts for the precipitate flight from being on the part of Western man, his progressive enslavement, the impoverishment of his life of feeling.

Modern man, his unity of self broken into fragments, seeks desperately to understand himself, his purpose on earth, the secret of being human. Science provided him with a vast storehouse of knowledge about the physical universe and showed him how to utilize its energy, but it taught him virtually nothing about his own being, so that gradually he lost the sense of his inner reality. Modern literature depicts him as if he were not truly alive, as if he were only a walking shadow in a dream within a dream.[5] If the tragic vision is to emerge, it must present a hero who fights against this fate of inner death.

iii

The Greek tragic writers, by affirming the fact of human responsibility, embodied an interpretation of man that is basically tragic. If they exalted the power and the pride of man, they also pointed out his insignificance in the total scheme of things. In relation to the cosmos he was but an atom, impotent before the mighty forces of nature that could destroy him. To balance this "pessimistic" view of human nature, they showed that man was endowed with imagination and intellect, which enabled him to rise above the limitations of his terrestrial environment. Out of this complex vision of existence they derived their conception of man as both heroic and pitiable. The tragic view of life they set forth in their plays offered no solution to the enigmatic questions it raised so energetically. The tragic view, in short, "elevates man from a worm to the status of a question mark." [6]

In Greek tragedy the hero suffers not without cause; he must be the responsible agent of his own undoing or he must toward the end of his ordeal be sufficiently enlightened to understand the truth about himself and therefore to accept the conditions that life imposes on mortal man. It is this attitude of acceptance which is missing in the testament of modern literature. As we saw in the previous chapter, the modern visionary, instead of resigning himself to the scheme of things and acknowledging his helplessness in the face of necessity, plunges into revolt. He knows he is nothing, but this "nothing" is all he has and he will make the most of it. He will not renounce the "divine" impulse in his being that bids him rebel rather than abase himself in fear and trembling before the mystery of existence.

The tragic vision today thus culminates in a naked revelation of self, without the affirmation of values that lie beyond the sphere of the natural. The absurd hero, who is absurd even when he rebels, struggles painfully but resolutely toward the goal of full disclosure. Nothing can deter him from this passionate commitment to the truth. This is the distinctive mark of his tragic consciousness: he forges ahead despite his knowledge that he can do nothing to alter his lot. There is no categorical imperative to be obeyed, no ultimate meaning to be pieced together, no cure for his dread. If he feels "guilty," it is not because he has transgressed against the laws of God but because he has violated his inner self or failed to keep faith with his fellow men, all of whom are victims of death but privileged beings for that very reason. Actually he does not, like the protagonist in *The Trial* or Meursault in *The Stranger*, feel guilty at all; his fate is thrust upon him without his will. The modern writer does not function like a justice of the Supreme Court, setting good and evil, right and wrong, in their proper categories. He seeks to understand and to reveal, while preserving all the ambivalent tentions of the world of reality. He is not a judge but "a justifier." [7]

The modern protagonist thus ceases to manifest any of the traditional virtues of "the heroic." The unheroic or anti-heroic hero makes his debut in the nineteenth century. Oblomov is born.[8] It is no longer a question of submitting to the will of the gods. The unheroic hero must assume sole responsibility for himself. The burden of Kafka's fiction is designed to show that man is unjustly punished. The curtain of the mystery is never lifted; the heavy and weary weight of all this unintelligible world is never lightened. When the hero of *A Farewell to Arms* escapes from the hell of war, he embraces the life of sensations, which is all he has or can have. He renounces the rhetoric of idealism for that which is beautifully concrete and real: road signs, food, the body of the woman he loves.

Hemingway, like Céline, depicts a world instinct with cruelty and destructive violence. His heroes are beset on all sides by hostile forces. The world will break them and those it cannot break it will kill. Hence in desperation they must grasp their physical pleasures while they can; always at their back they hear time's chariot hurrying near. All life has been turned into a battlefield. Death is the universal enemy of mankind. Whether the hero dies in bed in the fullness of years or is reduced to radioactive ashes in the atomic holocaust, his consciousness will be annulled and his body converted into inorganic matter, a stone, a leaf, a particle of dust. Life is a trap. No one ever gets away with anything. "You did not know what it was about. You never had time to learn. They threw you in and told you the rules and the first time they caught you off base they killed you. . . . You could count on that. Stay around and they would kill you." [9]

The modern unheroic hero may feel trapped in a universe of the absurd, but he refuses to subsist on illusions. Like Ahab, he will pierce straight through the mask of life. He is impelled by a passionate desire to find out who he really is. It is always man who makes tragedy meaningful. The tragic view brings into focus the conflict that never ceases between the lofty aspirations of man (the horizon of heaven) and the mutability of things (the hole in the ground that symbolizes his mortal element). The protagonist comes to understand at last that all life is doomed to suffer shipwreck, as the finite is swallowed up by the infinite. But if man has usurped the place of

The Tragic Hero 71

God, he does not know for what purpose he exists. All he knows is that he must choose his own reason for being. The Existentialist hero, a man without a self he can call his own, stands apart from Nature and yet it is Nature that is the ground of contingency. It is Nature which springs the trap in which he is caught, Nature which shuts him off from all possibilities of transcendence. As Gott-fried Benn points out, the phenotype of the present age is compounded of ambivalence. The ego has no stand-point.[10]

iv

The literary nihilist of our time has caught a vision of the reality of nothingness. The modern protago-nist realizes that he is the plaything of forces stronger than his reason or will. He knows that he does not know. Since all men are condemned to die, nothing is of any importance. He is reduced to a state of spiritual impo-tence, but he persists in seeking to grasp the truth at any cost. And the truth elicited, as in Samuel Beckett's ni-hilistic fiction, is that there is no meaning in the universe.

Beckett's chief passion is to "know," to "understand," even when he deliberately heightens the effect of tragi-comic irony. He uses characters as the medium through which to exhibit action, thought, introspection, and fan-tasy in a shadowy and weird universe. Perception is shown to be deceptive, consciousness is rebuffed in its efforts to penetrate the mystery of reality. Every event is seen to be not only ambiguous but inexplicable. Whereas Kafka treats the extraordinary as if it were the most com-mon occurrence, Beckett employs the reductive method of rationalism to demonstrate the phantasmagoric quality of existence. Beckett's characters are articulate abstrac-tions (of what value would individuation be in a time-space continuum that cannot satisfy the metaphysical hunger of man for the bread of meaning?) who question all that is usually taken for granted—birth, death, eating, sleeping, the routine of work, travel, what not. Man is crucified on the cross of unknowing, lost in the woods, waiting at a cross road in space for a Godot who will never come. The quest for meaning goes on in Beckett's world of the absurd, but it is a quest which, however filled with anguish, can never break out in revolt.

Beckett is a nihilist who beholds no glimmer of light, no ideal that is not smashed by contingency and annulled by death. He rejects humanity as a vain hypertrophied consciousness, a monstrous mistake. Life is a farcical ordeal. Faith is a delusion. All is conjecture. The disease of consciousness from which his characters suffer is designed to illustrate the pervasive theme of the absence of meaning.

Paul Bowles, too, is fascinated by the study of character types that have lost their identity. Though they have sufficient energy left to eat and drink and explore the delights of the flesh—sensuality is, as in Lawrence Durrell's fiction, one desperate means of negating the threat of death—they have no essential purpose in living. In *Let It Come Down,* the hero, lost in the middle of nowhere, feels superfluous on earth, prisoner of a destiny that is both tedious and meaningless. He lacks the will to shape his future; he cannot make things happen and yet, irrationally, he waits for something to happen. If he resorts to action, this represents a kind of random, ineffectual struggle to lose himself, to discover, as he says, a way out of the fly-trap. He does not know why he takes the trouble to sleep and wake. He comes close to himself only after he stops thinking of himself as heading in any given direction. "Because life is not a movement toward or away from anything; not even from the past to the future, or from youth to old age, or from birth to death. The whole of life does not equal the sum of its parts. It equals any of the parts; there is no sum." [11] It is foolish to look for reasons, a principle of justification for life. The hero, Dyar, has given up the struggle; he will be whatever he is.

But what is he? A simulacrum, a shadow, without any convictions to buoy him up. He simply exists. He is not really alive but dead. The thought of infinity fills him with horror. "If only existence could be cut down from the pinpoint of here and now, with no echoes reverberating from the past, no tinglings of expectation from time not yet arrived!" [12] He can find no sense in an everlasting present.

The Spider's House offers a brilliant contrast in depth between two cultures, that of the Moslem world, time-less, static, and fatalistic, and that of the West, dynamic, reformist, obsessed with the future. It is Stenham, the ex-Communist, a writer possessed of a quivering sensi-bility and acute powers of observation, who seems to voice the author's own values. Was man to obey Nature, as the Moslems believed, or try to control her? Stenham seeks to keep up with his writing, for that lends a sem-blance of meaning to his existence, but he cannot long silence his doubts as to the validity of his work. His crea-tive activity is an opiate distraction, merely a way of kill-ing time, and yet he is unable to discover any other rea-son for living. Having lost faith in both the Communist Party and in Marxism, he withdrew into the fastness of his own subjectivity. "Nothing had importance save the exquisitely isolated cosmos of his own consciousness." [13] The meaning of everything in the world was dying. In short, he felt that all existence, including his own, "had become absurd and unreal." [14]

Bowles' work underlines the familiar Existentialist re-frain: man is not an essence. He is what he does with his life. The hero in Bowles' fiction can do nothing with his life; he cannot save himself and he has given up the desire to save the world. Deprived of a unified self, the Existen-tialist hero overthrows the tyranny of reason and faces the ineradicable ambiguity of existence.[15] He looks for no ultimate solutions. He must take action even though ev-erything is "unreal." That is the dilemma he confronts: life is absurd! He must learn to live without relying on hope. He is free to act but this very freedom is the source of his anguish. He is estranged from himself. He is drawn resistlessly toward a future that will annihilate his present self and bring about his death. He is henceforth alone and his only mark of grandeur, a negative virtue, lies in his unwillingness to blind himself to the misery of existence in a universe of the absurd.

The tragic hero of the twentieth century demands too much of life and too much of himself. All or nothing! He cannot have all and he refuses to reconcile himself to nothing. Life is his only assured value, but even that may at any instant be taken away from him. He transcends nihilism and becomes a truly tragic figure when he comes to realize that it is not life itself he cherishes but life on terms that conform to his conception of what is honorable and just, even if these "ideals" are freely chosen, not supported by the physical universe he inhabits. The sensuous beauty of the earth, the pleasures of immediacy, these alone cannot hold him. He strives to become an authentic self. He insists on asking for the light of meaning by which he can guide his life. If there is no absolute meaning, he will create his own human meaning. It is this unrelenting will to truth which is one of the distinctive features of the modern tragic vision. If he lacks the rebellious freedom to affirm his being, he is only a victim of cruel circumstances; he ceases to be tragic. If the odds against him, as in Beckett's world, are so overwhelming that he does not stand a chance, then all we get is an intolerably heightened feeling of nihilistic futility. The protagonist who fittingly embodies the tragic vision must possess, or act as if he possessed, freedom of choice. It is a form of freedom which he finds it supremely difficult to sustain in a scientific universe.

Ideology and Tragedy

THE TRAGIC VISION AND
THE SCIENTIFIC SYNTHESIS

IT IS ALWAYS the nature of man that is basic to the tragic vision. But the mechanistic theory of life, by refusing to acknowledge the existence of the uncaused and the unconditional, deprives man of his birthright of freedom. He is transformed into a machine. Here is a view of life, according to one biologist, that needs "a poet inspired to a red-hot enthusiasm by the inflexible laws of the atom, by the unshakeable determinism of physico-chemical explanations, and by the exquisite harmonies and adjustments of which pure physico-chemical systems are capable." [1] The fact remains that no modern poet, not even a Robinson Jeffers or a Hart Crane, has been inspired to a red-hot enthusiasm by the inflexible laws of the atoms or the determinism of physico-chemical systems. The mechanistic hypothesis turns man into an organism that functions like a machine, and there is nothing tragic in a machine or in the machinery of fate. It is the advance of science, according to a number of influential critics, which has been chiefly responsible for the death of tragedy. In the past, man felt that he was in intimate relationship with the laws or powers that govern the universe. Now that science is the dominant world outlook, tragedy can no longer portray man as a godlike protagonist in the cosmic order of things.

Though the scientific outlook may account for the virtual disappearance of tragedy that conforms to the ancient Greek model, the tragic spirit endures and makes itself today strongly felt. But it operates within a predominantly secular, relativistic context. The ideology that supported the tragic drama of the past has fallen apart.[2] The focus of tragic heroism shifts from the locus of theology to that of history and society. The modern hero has ceased to be, or so he believes, a fool of time and nature. The metaphysical presuppositions that once offered such ennobling sources of consolation have been cast off; science has provided new forms of belief. It remains to be seen whether these beliefs could be reconciled with the principle of opposition invariably present in the tragic vision, the metaphysical urge that impels man to affirm his moral freedom and the meaningfulness of his existence.

The nineteenth century struggled desperately to formulate a method of reconciliation between Darwinism and the teachings of Christianity. If Darwin's scientific data and the conclusions drawn from them were valid, then the theory of a divine agency in the process of creation would have to be abandoned. If species, in response to environmental conditions, changed in the course of time, then all this had nothing to do with God or the soul. *The Origin of Species* shattered the anthropomorphic conceit of Homo sapiens, though Darwin continued to insist that there was grandeur in the doctrine of natural selection.

The writers in the second half of the nineteenth century found little or no grandeur in it, nor could they feel at home in a universe of matter which had no place for moral values. They could not affirm their belief in the immortal destiny of man when the species to which he belonged emerged accidentally in the spawning process of biological evolution. Why did he deserve a degree of eminence not accorded to the worm or the ant? He knew now—and he had to learn to live with this knowledge— his absolute nullity in space and time. Writers were thus drawn to science, which was a source of Promethean power, and yet repelled by its abstract formulas. Like Dostoevski's underground man, they could not resign themselves to a universe that functioned like a machine.

They had in some way to come to terms with the scientific revolution. They had to overcome the fear that science would gradually conquer all of life. Many were dismayed by the laws of physics, especially The Second Law of Thermodynamics, which pictured the eventual "death by freezing" of the entire universe.[3] These were the conflicts that gripped the minds of such writers as Kierkegaard, Dostoevski, Nietzsche, Tolstoy, Hardy, O'Neill, Sartre, and Camus. Hardy embraced the major ideas of nineteenth-century science. There were times when he envied those who possessed a simple, all-inclusive faith, but he could not share it. As far as he was concerned, the First Cause, however it be named, is without consciousness, operating nonrationally. It is this power which controls the universe blindly. The Prime Mover is an automaton, which works without plan, logic, or intelligence. Man is at the mercy of chance and fate. All he can know is that he is born and that he dies. There is no sense in brooding everlastingly on the meaning of life.[4] No systematic thinker, Hardy interpreted life by personifying the forces, whatever they were, which governed the flux of energy in the universe. In the beginning he looked upon these forces as the operation of blind chance or crass casualty, what Sartre calls "contingency." Not until later did there emerge the Schopenhauerian principle of the Immanent Will.

Hardy, in his fiction and poetry, anticipates many of the conflicts, precipitated by the scientific world view, that found their way into twentieth-century literature. He portrayed the indifference of Nature to moral values. It works without regard for human desires. In *The Dynasts*, he dealt with the problem of cosmic injustice, the existence of useless suffering. In the timeless vision of the Spirit of the Years, Christianity appears to be no more than an insignificant and ephemeral cult among the suns and planets in space. The First Cause, never identified as God, is called by a variety of neutral names: "the Prime Mover of the Gear," "the Prime Volition," "the One," "the Immanent," "this all-inhering Power," "the Immanent Shaper," "the Mighty Will," "the Unknowable," and so on.[5] God becomes a mechanism, a force that stands for the Unknowable, dark and dumb, without consciousness or personality. Science, not Nietzsche, had slain God.

According to some critics, it also hastened the death of tragedy. George Steiner, in *The Death of Tragedy*, declares that "tragedy is that form of art which requires the intolerable burden of God's presence. It is now dead because His shadow no longer falls upon us as it fell on Agamemnon or Macbeth or Athalie."[6] Both of these assumptions are rejected by those modern writers who, without the intolerable burden of God's presence, have built the architecture of the tragic vision. The new form of tragedy is not only possible in our time; it has been produced by such men as Faulkner, Malraux, O'Neill, Sartre, and Camus.

ii

The difficulties that block the release of the tragic vision in an age that is dominated by the scientific world view are admittedly great but they are not insuperable. Man, it is true, cannot face his destiny with any measure of freedom when he regards himself as only a biological accident. At the mercy of the complex industrial civilization the scientific revolution has brought into being, he dwells in a cultural climate that makes skepticism mandatory and absolute. The "New Philosophy" has brought everything into doubt, even infecting him with the enervating suspicion that life on earth is without ultimate meaning. The hegemony of science marked the triumph in literature of a nihilism that had to be voiced even while the writer struggled to transcend it. Nietzsche pointed out how this could be done. While science classifies phenomena and predicts how they will behave, reality remains phantasmal and truth unattainable.[7] Physics discloses an absolute reality that is conceptual, dematerialized, enigmatic. "Nature turns into a network of concepts and symbols, and these in turn produce matter and Nature."[8] In such a phantom world, incapable of apprehending truth objectively, the best the mind can is to create its own values, knowing they are human values.

The development of science thus threw man on his own resources. It conferred on him a marvellous degree of control over his physical environment, but it also forced him to acknowledge his own total insignificance. There is nothing tragic in the scientific outlook. It is astonishing to find Whitehead contending that fate in Greek tragedy anticipates the order of Nature revealed in modern science. Not that he felt there was any force in the analogy beyond the single point of resemblance: the discernible pattern of uniformity in the processes of Nature. It was this resemblance which led him to say: "The laws of physics are the decrees of fate." [9] Science is ethically neutral and therefore neither tragic nor antitragic. It pictures an abstract, dehumanized universe of electrons, protons, genes, gamma rays, wave particles, nuclear energy.

Whereas Zola, in his essay on naturalism in the theatre, felt that he was in possession of a radically new method of representation, a scientific analysis of character that could furnish a true portrayal of "reality," D. H. Lawrence simply refused to accept the scientific explanation of life. What could it contribute but a confusing series of abstractions. The individual, he argued, was the supreme fact, the miracle not to be contravened by any scientific formula. "There never was any universe, any cosmos, of which the first reality was anything but living, incorporate individuals." [10] Philosophically more literate in their revolt against science, a number of modern writers decided to accept the mysterious irrationality of things and events. Things are what they seem, not as science represents them diagrammatically. Rebelling against the limitations of scientific rationalism, men like Gide, Camus, Malraux, and Sartre give us the first full disclosure of the reality of the absurd.

Waging a difficult struggle to capture a reality that has not been mediated by thought, the poet must return to the purity of things in themselves. Even as his consciousness burns with a brighter flame and his aesthetic sensibility is intensified, he is always aware of the incomprehensible universe outside of him, the radical incommensurability of mind and matter, the human and the nonhuman. Here is the central source of the modern sense of the tragic: "the exterior world is overwhelming and absurd, but there is no refuge from it." [11] This is the paradox inherent in the modern sense of the tragic. While it hastened the emancipation of the senses from the tyranny of concepts, it nevertheless bore witness to the triumph of science. The exquisite harmonies and adjustments of which pure physico-chemical systems are capable had driven home the tragic truth of the absurd.

This did not mean that man could find no way of escape out of his hermetically sealed prison of subjectivity or that he would have to adjust himself, stoically or defiantly, to a world that was incorrigibly absurd. If that were the case, the modern writer could achieve no outlet for the tragic vision. The Existentialist declares that man is what he makes of himself. The individual stands forth anew in his freedom. Scientific determinism had stripped him of the assurance that his will was free. Existentialism gave him back this forfeited sense of freedom. It is his task to construct the order of the world he lives in. There are no scientific absolutes to which he must submit. There are no higher laws, no ultimate meaning; the universe is simply there. Absurdity reigns, but the Existentialist hero is the one who is "condemned" to be free. He does not foist his guilt on some anonymous scapegoat, society or the unconscious or the indifference of the universe. With profound irony Sartre shows in his plays and novels how the heart of motivation is to be found in the paradox of freedom, which is also the paradox of tragedy. If the tragic hero is convinced from the start that he is doomed by forces he cannot hope to control, then he can never come to grips with his destiny. The great tragedies are those in which the outcome is brought about by the protagonist's decision to assert his moral freedom.

O'Neill, a child of his century, wrestled with the problem of fate in a world governed by universal determinism.

If he was profoundly influenced by Nietzsche's Dionysian conception of tragedy as a celebration of life despite all its horrors, he could not rest content with a purely aesthetic resolution of the mystery of existence. As he wrote in 1925:

> I'm always acutely conscious of the Force behind (Fate, God, our biological past creating our present, whatever one calls it, Mystery certainly)—and of the one eternal tragedy of Man in his glorious, self-destructive struggle to make the Force express him instead of being, as an animal is, an infinitesimal incident in its expression. And my proud conviction is that this is the only subject worth writing about and that it is possible—or can be—to develop a tragic expression in terms of transfigured modern values and symbols in the theatre which may to some degree bring home to members of a modern audience their ennobling identity with the tragic figures on the stage.[12]

This revealing confession is in line with our thesis that tragedy is not dead; it seeks expression "in terms of transfigured modern values and symbols." The statement discloses the tenacity with which O'Neill as a dramatist pursued the metaphysical quest for ultimate meaning in a universe which worships the new God of science. He invokes Fate, the biological past, the pervading sense of Mystery, and then points out that the human struggle, however glorious, is self-destructive.

Like the tragic writers of the past, O'Neill insists that man must give up his romantic illusions. Like Dreiser, he is convinced that there is no shadow of correspondence between what the heart desires and what man finally achieves. Though he pictured the universe as essentially unmoral, he never exalted science as offering mankind the road to salvation. Life is an end in itself. Man is free to forge his own destiny. He must accept life on naturalistic terms, though O'Neill's haunted heroes cannot abandon the quest for meaning. Even Yank, a profane, hairy stoker on a transatlantic liner, is filled with this urgent craving to relate himself to a universe of meaning, to make the Force, whatever one calls it, express him, but the spiritual home he yearns for is not to be found. O'Neill in this play sounds the theme of man struggling futilely with his own fate, crushed by the weight of things, unable to appeal to the gods for deliverance. In some respects, O'Neill's version of the human struggle is similar to the one Sartre sets forth in his Existentialist tragedies.[13]

A part of Nature that refuses to merge with it, man is now at odds with his environment, driven out of the paradise of innocence by the sharpened sword of scientific reason. He is at war with himself, the biological pitted against the human, the instinctual against the spiritual. *Strange Interlude* deals, like *Dynamo*, with the conflict between the absolutism of religion and the absolutism of science. After the death of her puritanical father, Nina Leeds had tried to pray "to the modern science God. I thought of a million light years to a spiral nebula—one other universe among innumerable others. But how could that God care about our trifling misery of death-born-of-birth? I couldn't believe in Him, and I wouldn't if I could! I'd rather imitate His indifference and prove I had that one trait in common." [14] She cannot believe—that is her tragedy. At the end, her lover, his dream of happiness ended, cries out: "Oh, God, so deaf and dumb and blind! . . . teach me to be resigned to be an atom!" [15]

O'Neill's tragedies show that man can never be resigned to be an atom. The tragic vision is eclipsed if the hero is denied the freedom that spurs him on to rebel against blind necessity. Nevertheless, it cannot cut itself off from scientific knowledge which is interested in all things. Universal in range, science seeks to dissipate the last vestiges of mystery, but it cannot solve the mystery of human existence or rob man entirely of his gift of freedom, however equivocal or limited it proves in action. It simply confirms the existential "truth" of the tragic vision, namely, that there is no final solution for the riddle of life.

THE MODERN WRITER is subjected to a host of influences so varied and complex that he is sometimes at a loss how to assimilate them into an ordered, harmonious whole. Freudianism, Marxism, relativity, nuclear physics, Existentialism: these are some of the competing perspectives which must be brought into meaningful unity if he is to give birth to an interpretation of life, tragic or not, that he regards as "true." [1] The Freudian doctrine made its influence felt on the modern literary scene. Prophetic figures like Kierkegaard, Dostoevski, Nietzsche, and Strindberg anticipated many of the insights that Freud later presented in his work. [2] What Freud did in his *Interpretation of Dreams*, published in 1900, was to lend the mighty warrant of science to his analysis of the mechanism of the dream. His concept of the unconscious served to turn the tide of interest from the current preoccupation with the psychology of consciousness. Here was a science that painted a new portrait of the nature of man, instinct-ridden, profoundly irrational. Freud, however, though he uncovered the irrational that governed the personality, remained militantly rationalistic in his system. [3]

It is this monistic rationalism which led a number of writers, Sartre among them, to rebel against the psychological determinism which lies at the base of the Freudian outlook. Freud made known a number of exciting things about the secrets of the creative process, [4] the logic of the dream, the operation of the unconscious, the stream-of-consciousness technique, [5] the relation of art to disease.

He brought to light many of the neurotic tendencies active in Western culture—its repressive function, its fear of sexuality, its craving for illusion, its ingrained hostility to truths that are painful. But his positivistic conception of reality, as opposed to the pleasure principle, relegated art to the sphere of illusion. Art, even tragic art, was rooted in sexuality. What the poet does is to utilize the forms of phantasy to gratify his instinctual wishes vicariously. Through his work he manages to overcome his neurosis.[6] It is this aspect of the Freudian system which makes it fundamentally antitragic.

Freud himself set an example of courageous devotion to the scientific truth, wherever it might lead, regardless of the envenomed opposition of his society. What drew him to the study of medicine and then to psychoanalysis was the overpowering need "to understand something of the riddles of the world in which we live and perhaps even to contribute something to their solution."[7] Bold Faustian ambition, this was the motive which led him to become the spiritual mentor and father confessor of mankind. He spared the race none of its deep-seated illusions, its religious hopes, its high-minded principles of universal justice. "Dark, unfeeling and unloving powers determine human destiny; the system of rewards and punishments, which, according to religion, governs the world, seems to have no existence."[8] But Freud, symbol of Promethean man, would not submit to these dark, unfeeling, and unloving powers. He never relinquished his faith that science was the indispensable method available to humanity if it wished to gain some rational control over reality.[9] The only hope for the future—and Freud cherished this hope despite his pessimistic pronouncements in *The Future of an Illusion*—lay in allowing the scientific spirit to guide the human mind. "Where id was, there shall ego be."[10]

Freudianism thus carried forward, on a scientific basis, the work of ideological demolition begun by Nietzsche. It stripped man of his faith in the existence of God. Naturalistic in his orientation, Freud devoted himself single-mindedly to the task of liberating mankind from the clutch of blind instinct and neurotic illusion. Steadfastly he labored to make man sufficiently self-reliant, through the knowledge gained from empirically tested disciplines, to accept the burden of his finite biological destiny. If he rejected the foundations on which super- natural religion is based, he believed in the supreme value of truth. Hence his endeavor to formulate a "science" of the mind. But his metapsychology was not without its mythic and ethical ingredients. Life is the triumph, daily renewed, of Eros over Thanatos, the primary death in- stinct. Because in the midst of life men are surrounded by death, "All that is living must be loving so as not to die." [11]

Exciting as it proved in its exploration of the dark Congo of the unconscious, the Freudian system, which is supported by its own metaphysical presuppositions, left the modern writer a legacy of unresolved conflicts and contradictions. It condemned the metaphysical urge in man as born of illusion, but it is this very "illusion" that constitutes the archetypal theme of tragedy. The hero who is in essence nothing but a bundle of instincts is little better off than the hero who, as in Kafka's fiction, is re- duced to a thing or an insect. The subjective feeling of freedom is a psychologically real datum. There can be no tragic conflict that does not rest on the concept of free will. In an extreme situation, such as Karl Jaspers describes in *Tragedy Is Not Enough*, the hero sets out on his jour- ney through the dark night of the soul [12] and is defeated in his quest for meaning, but his failure is a glorious vindication of his humanity, his courage to be.

There is a tragic grandeur in Freud's view of life as ruled by the death instinct, but on the whole his concep- tion of reality and the nature of man was too restricted to serve the needs of writers. Whereas Freud sought to make the ego prevail over the id, they discovered in the uncon- scious, the source of the mysterious and the perverse, a potent weapon to use against the laws of reason. Many of them ignored his determinism. It was in the name of existential freedom that Sartre rejected not only the theory of the unconscious but, in effect, the whole of Freudian determinism. Man chooses his own motivations, the values he will abide by, and thus shapes his own world. This freedom of choice removes him from the iron grip of environmental determinism. The goal he chooses for himself (Sartre shows how this worked out in the case of Baudelaire) determines the rest of his life.[13] The unconscious, Sartre holds, is anchored in the past while psychological, like environmental, determinism affords man a way of lying to himself and dwelling in "bad faith." All behavior, Sartre believes, is purposive and free. Man is not only an object among objects but an incarnation of the potentialities of freedom not to be found in Nature, in things-in-themselves. A man must be not only what he is; he must at the same time be able to become what he is not, constantly remaking himself.[14]

The insistence of the Freudian system that all human behavior was rigidly determined worked havoc with the writer's approach to the tragic vision. Once the psychic as well as the physical universe is transformed into a closed causal system, then the possibilities of tragic affirmation are sealed off. Within a deterministic world, the tragic hero is utterly prevented from reaching out toward the goal of self-transcendence. The tragic vision, whatever insoluble ambiguities and enigmas it may propound, is committed of necessity to the metaphysical principle that man is a free agent. It is the signal virtue of existential analysis, a rebellious offshoot from the parent stock of Freudianism, that it is steadily aware of the tragic sense of life. A dynamic approach to psychiatry, derived largely from the work of Heidegger and in part from that of Kierkegaard, it throws a new light on the problematical nature of man. Unlike the Freudian method, it does not treat mental illness as the product of a specific syndrome but as the result of the patient's balked efforts to discover a viable meaning in life. The patient, like all of us, struggles to find a genuine meaning in life so that his existence can once more become positive and purposive.[15] Energetically moving in the direction of the goals it has chosen, the human personality pushes beyond the scope of biological development, beyond nature, in a quest for transcendence.

Existential analysis furnishes a more complex revelation

of the reality of the self and the subjective "truth" of experience. Reacting against the tendency of a mechanistic psychology to dichotomize life into subject and object, it seeks to restore sensory experience to its place of primary importance. (This is, of course, precisely what writers like D. H. Lawrence, Hemingway, Malraux, and Faulkner have done.) It postulates a basic qualitative distinction between knowing and experiencing.[16] As its contributions become better known, existential analysis may help to enrich the literature of the tragic vision.[17]

None of the writers who were influenced by Freudianism—D. H. Lawrence, Sherwood Anderson, Arthur Koestler, Eugene O'Neill, and Tennessee Williams—were interested in its scientific implications. They took what they needed for their creative purpose and boldly modified whatever insights they borrowed. Though they were aware of the determinism that characterizes tragic action, playwrights like O'Neill presented characters who are not completely at the mercy of their instincts or their unconscious. They are endowed with some measure of free will.

Pre-Freudian in his dramaturgy, Strindberg takes up, particularly in his expressionistic plays, the quest of lonely tormented souls for the meaning of life. The unities of time and place are cast aside. In his preface to *A Dream Play*, Strindberg declares: "Anything can happen; everything is possible and probable. Time and space do not exist." [18] The sense of life is limited to the consciousness of the dreamer, a subjectivity that does not condemn but simply reveals. Strindberg is modern in his disintegration of the classical forms of tragedy. His work, like that of Ibsen, illustrates the collapse of the old rational world order and the mythological values it called forth. The eye of the imagination is now focused broodingly on the inferno of the private soul. Strindberg sets the stage for the emergence of new forms of the tragic vision.

ii

Throughout his life Strindberg felt bitter and isolated, estranged from his country and its culture, the victim of periodic hallucinations, doubting the reality of the world and his own self. Here was the dramatist who undertook to portray the spiritual disorders of his age, but he also strove to shadow forth the mysterious element in life itself. He gave expression to the compulsions of the irrational, the sense of the uncanny, the feeling of dread. Small wonder he was deeply moved by the writings of Kierkegaard. When he was asked what power he would most like to wield, he replied that it was the power to solve the riddle of the sphinx.

Though he belonged to his age, he went far beyond its spirit of scientific rationalism in dealing with the chaos of the unconscious. In wrestling with the phantoms of his mind and projecting them as living figures on the stage, he left behind him the deterministic assumptions of the naturalists. The life he reveals is no longer tidy, but turbulent, incoherent, even violent in its upsurge of demonic forces. All is flux, mutability, contradiction. His naturalistic and expressionistic dramas were attempts to come to terms with Darwinism. They were, according to one critic, "the two archetypal patterns of defeat in the modern world: defeat at the hands of a naturalistic nihilism and defeat at the hands of a compensatory supernaturalism." [19] With clairvoyant insight Strindberg delineated the atomistic break-up of the human personality into a battlefield of mutually incompatible and antagonistic forces.

Even in his naturalistic plays, he focused attention on the revelations of the unconscious mind. *Miss Julie,* a naturalistic tragedy, shows how a woman belonging to the aristocratic order is dragged under by the tyranny of sex. It is in his expressionistic plays, however, that Strindberg employed most effectively the technique of objectifying inner states, the turbid conflicts of the unconscious. His Expressionism endeavors to find a dramatic correlative for the archetypal quest of man for the absolute. It uses heightened subjectivity as a means of transcending the abstract world of concepts fashioned by science. It reports mystical visions and transformations wrought by the power of dream and fantasy. A *Dream Play* discloses a world that is inconceivable in terms of reason, a world compounded of irrational desires and nameless nostalgias.

What unites the characters in Strindberg's expressionistic dramas, who possess no fixed identity, is the consciousness of the dreamer. Each one is alone and inscrutably complex, even to himself. There are locked doors and no one knows what is behind them. Nothing turns out as these characters had expected. All of them live on illusions, which cannot ever be fulfilled on earth. Humanity has made a mess of life. Existence is a meaningless affliction; people keep on asking the same foolish and futile questions until death mercifully supervenes. The worst part of living, as in the tragedies composed by the ironic but always compassionate Chekhov, is the experience of stale, endless repetition. When the door is finally opened, nothing can be seen—nothing! Despite his strong mystical leanings in his later period, Strindberg voices a nihilism that no compensatory supernaturalism can overcome. Suffering, as in Sophoclean tragedy, fails to bring wisdom. The only purpose it serves is to liberate mankind from the earth-bound trammels of illusion.

The Spook Sonata, in going beyond the limits of strict representationalism, frees itself from the circle of psychological determinism. In a play like *The Dance of Death*, the first part of which was written in 1901, Strindberg explores one of his obsessive themes, the hell that is marriage as he knew it, the hatred, linked with love, that rises to a crescendo of murderous fury. The Captain and his wife are incapable of breaking the ties that bind them. Nothing but death can separate them and they are both impatiently waiting for this deliverance. The Captain cannot make out the meaning of life. Is it merely a superlative joke? In *The Road to Damascus*, Strindberg shows that not even love, the supreme illusion, can reconcile The Stranger, the protagonist who strongly resembles the author, to life. In Part III The Stranger at last makes up his mind and enters the monastery, but for Strindberg himself the renunciation that Christianity demanded offered no solution. He is among the first of the moderns to demonstrate how enormously difficult is the task of the writer today who wishes to make any tragic affirmation. Catastrophic suffering strikes blindly and affects everyone, without bringing any redemptive knowledge or wisdom. The belief in moral retribution or equity has been abandoned. The demonic forces of destruction that have been unleashed in the world must be combated within the individual psyche. In the modern tragic vision, human consciousness voices its protest, but it is unable to transcend the absurdity of existence. As Herbert Read declares: "We now have all the essential pre-requisites of tragedy—a sense of human misery—and we have a complete understanding of how tragedy should work. All we lack is tragedy." [20] Eugene O'Neill struggled valiantly to supply that lack.

iii

O'Neill admired Strindberg greatly and was influenced by his expressionistic techniques, but the vision of life he worked out is uniquely his own. In *Long Day's Journey into Night*, written in 1940, he reveals the tragic conditioning of his past, the crucial experiences which made him resemble one of the "haunted" heroes of his own plays. Autobiographical in content, this play, as he says in his dedication to his wife, was composed in tears and blood. It is a tragedy that discloses how each of the characters in the Tyrone family comes to understand himself in the light of events that took place in the past. Edmund, in particular, faces the meaning of his own existence, his estrangement from the universe, his sense of aloneness, his contingency. He is half in love with death because he can find no principle that will justify his life.

Gradually we begin to comprehend the forces that contributed to the breakdown of the Mother, who has become addicted to drugs. In moments of lucid insight she comes to realize that no one is responsible for what happened. The past made them what they are. Jamie, the older brother, believes that life is a frame-up; no one can hope to beat the game. When the father, who never goes to church, exalts the true faith of the Catholic Church, his younger son quotes Nietzsche to the effect that God is dead. The Mother sadly points out that the past is the present and the future, too. There is no way out.

In the last act, we see Tyrone defeated in the struggle, knowing he has lost. Edmund, who represents O'Neill himself, pours out all his accumulated store of bitterness. O'Neill denies that people want to face life as it is. He once tried to commit suicide at Jimmie the Priest's when, cold sober, he was confronting the truth about himself.

Thus in his last period O'Neill returned to his central theme of the battle against fate in which the outcome is foredoomed. The protagonist, stripped of all illusion, faces his authentic self, and we get, as in *The Iceman Cometh*, the tragedy of unmitigated despair. As a determinist, O'Neill dealt with situations in which men were plunged into disaster through no fault of their own. On whom, then, was the burden of responsibility to be placed? All O'Neill could reply was that men are destined to suffer without reason—a nihilistic motif that recurs again and again in our study of the tragic vision. The quest for meaning on earth is futile. Man is unable to feel that he belongs on this planet, which is his home. And yet the mind continues to thirst after God as the symbol of ultimate meaning, regardless of the fact that objectively no hint of purpose could be discerned. Man seeks to control his fate but his unconscious pulls him in different directions and frustrates his effort to impose order upon the chaotic flux of experience. There, in the unconscious, slumber the archetypal images of the gods, the gods who foil all attempts at the conscious governance of human destiny.

Early in his career, O'Neill was drawn to characters who were "possessed," fighting against themselves and the illusions they harbor. *The Great God Brown* is a tragedy which discloses the deep cleavage in the soul of O'Neill. Dion Anthony represents the artist in America, split within, alone, misunderstood, tormented by spiritual longings which he cannot fulfill. At the end Cybel, the prostitute, symbol of Mother Earth, proclaims the Dionysian theme of life's renewal, the undying flow of energy in the universe. O'Neill was struggling desperately hard to grasp the essential truth of life, however terrible its import. As the hero of *Welded*, a playwright, cries out: "To learn to love the truth of life—to accept it and be exalted—that's the one faith left to us!" [21]

O'Neill went further than Strindberg in seeking to reconcile the will to truth and the treacherous machinations of the unconscious. Unlike Strindberg, he never turned mystical or "religious," with the single exception of *Days Without End*. He entertained no hopes, however, that science could give him the solution his skeptical mind craved. Freudianism, like the contributions of Jung, could illuminate some of the hidden motives of the psyche, but it could not possibly answer the existential questions which a playwright like O'Neill raised. Indeed, he denied that he consciously used psychoanalytic material in any of his plays.

> All of them could easily have been written by a dramatist who had never heard of the Freudian theory and was simply guided by an intuitive psychological insight into human beings and their life impulses that is as old as Greek drama. It is true that I am enough of a student of modern psychology to be fairly familiar with the Freudian implications inherent in the actions of some of my characters while I was portraying them; but this was always an afterthought and never consciously was I for a moment influenced to shape my material along the lines of any psychological theory. It was my dramatic insight and my own personal experiences with human life that alone guided me.[22]

This is substantially true, but the fact remains that in 1927, when he was writing *Strange Interlude*, he was undergoing analysis in order to be cured of his alcoholism. The play embodies many of the principal motifs of Freudian psychology: the relationship to the Mother, hostility toward the Father, the revolt of the instincts against the domination of the intellect, the incidence of neurosis, the fearful clutch of the past.[23] At the end, the realization on the part of Ned Darrell, the eugenic lover, that it is dangerous to interfere in human lives brings home the degree to which O'Neill deviated from Freudian orthodoxy. O'Neill valued the light psychoanalysis shed on the irrational component in man, the shattering impact of neuroses on the lives of human beings, but, like D. H. Lawrence, he is convinced that no scientific discipline can explain the soul of man.

In *Mourning Becomes Electra*, which provides a modern setting for the Orestes story, the neuroses of the Mannon family constitute their fate. The family pattern shapes the downfall of Ezra (Agamemnon), Christine (Clytemnestra), Lavinia (Electra), and Orin (Orestes). The Freudian interpretation of the characters is intended to show the effect of the Oedipus complex on Orin and the Electra complex on Lavinia.[24] The tragedy hinges on the psychological motivation of the individual characters. The gods play no part in determining the outcome. Nor does the play exhibit the vindication of any moral order. After the murder of her lover, Adam Brant (Aegisthus), Christine, hunted and desperate, cries out: "Why can't all of us remain innocent and loving and trusting? But God won't leave us alone. He twists and wrings and tortures our lives with others' lives—until we poison each other to death!"[25] Only it is not God who has done this to them, it is their own neurotic fixations. There is no escape for Christine or Orin or Lavinia from the consequences of their own guilt. The dead do not die; they live on to haunt the living who are guilty. Instead of asking God or society for forgiveness, Lavinia declares: "I forgive myself!"[26] Though the dead come between her and her dream of happiness, she will not, like Orin, commit suicide. She must punish herself. "Living alone here with the dead is a worse act of justice than death or prison! . . . I'll live alone with the dead, and keep their secrets, and let them hound me, until the curse is paid out and the last Mannon is let die!"[27]

The hero trapped in his neuroses never reaches the tragic heights. Blindly he rushes ahead to capture the will-o'-the-wisp of happiness, only to be thwarted by his own neuroses. O'Neill at his tragic best is not at all Freudian in his resolution. Freedom versus fate, the spirit fighting, always in vain, to transcend instinct, the dead weight of the meaningless opposed to the human need to impose order on the universe, the pull of the unconscious undermining the ideals they pursue: this is the paradox of the tragic vision that O'Neill explores in his work. This paradox is brought out with greater sharpness and deeper complexity of insight in the work of Jean-Paul Sartre.

EXISTENTIALISM AND
THE TRAGIC VISION

> The atheist doesn't bother about God because he had
> made up his mind once for all that God doesn't exist.[1]

THE PHILOSOPHY OF Sartrean Existentialism has a direct
and important bearing on the structure of the tragic vision
as it emerges in Sartre's fiction and dramas. If there is
anything disturbingly new in Existentialism it is not "the
doctrine" per se, the phenomenological ontology set forth
in *Being and Nothingness*, but the febrile intensity with
which it stresses the theme of alienation, the nothingness
of man vis-a-vis the universe and the necessity he is under
to affirm his freedom, the psychology of "bad faith." Freedom—that is the single, obsessive burden of its message.
Man's freedom is inescapable and manifests itself in each
of the choices he makes. Freedom is what one is, even
though it functions always within a given situation.
Though existential psychoanalysis appropriates a number
of basic ideas from the Freudian system in its interpretation of psychic life, the differences in point of view are
fundamental. What Sartre repudiates is the emphasis
Freudian psychology places on determinism. He rejects
the explanation of psychic life in terms of instinct, he rejects hereditary and constitutional factors as the shaping
influence on character,[2] and he rejects the theory of an
unconscious. This is the psychological determinism that
he discards completely.

A revolt against abstract systems of thought, Existentialism projects a *Weltanschauung* that is rooted in the actual existence of the individual. Existence cannot be reduced to a system. Never! Behind every philosophical construction, however "objective" in its terminology, there is heard the voice of the anguished being who speaks. It cannot be otherwise. The Existentialist will allow neither the counters of abstract thought nor the oppression of *Angst* to stifle his spontaneity of being or his determined quest for the truth. Confronting life in all its contingency and contradictions, he accepts the challenge of subjectivity. Reality is not to be defined in terms of the objects that comprise it. Existence, in short, is not only indefinable but inexhaustible.

It is this ontological struggle which can never be abandoned and never prove successful that underlies the tragic vision of Existentialist literature. Everything in the universe is a mystery, and the greatest mystery of all is the fact of consciousness: the awareness of man of his fate at this juncture of time and space, the knowledge he possesses of the irreducible irrationality of existence. He exists but his existence cannot be justified. It does not make sense. Repeatedly Sartre develops the theme that the human being has no particular business on earth.

Though Existentialism heightens the gratuitousness and absurdity of the human situation, it portrays existence as a perpetually renewed crisis of consciousness. The Existentialist hero achieves no stasis of certitude, no triumphant epiphany, yet he refuses to give up the fight. That is the meaning of "the nausea" which afflicts him: the ontological wound from which he bleeds gives rise, through suffering, to no miracle of reconciliation. Even as he strives to assert his freedom and lead what he considers an authentic existence, he knows the uselessness of his struggle. The only thing he can look forward to is the prospect of dying. That is why Heidegger defines *Dasein* as Being-toward-death. Every moment of life is a dying; everything man does is but a vain effort to escape from the ignominious destiny of death.

Sartre carries the metaphysics of revolt to its farthest limits. Though man is pure subjectivity, his existence is in society. It is social reality that is primary. The individual is influenced in his way of life by the dominant philosophies of the culture he lives in. Hence an ideology is no superstructure; it is a foundation that determines how the individual conducts his own life. Sartre's plays, like his novels, illustrate the difficult struggle the modern writer must wage in adapting his tragic vision of life to the ideological pressures of his age. Not that men respond to their world in terms of metaphysical concepts. They live and then they think. They do not possess a common nature. A general definition of man is an impossibility.

This conception of man is basic to Sartre's ontology and is exemplified in the character of his tragic heroes. Reason must not be exalted as paramount in the quest for knowledge. Logic is no longer the open sesame to the heart of reality. The irrational must be taken into account. Existence comes first. Each man, however circumscribed by his historical and environmental situation, is the author of his own life. He is "here," on this earth, "now," never able to find out why things are as they are. No law of necessity hems him in. From the viewpoint of his consciousness, existence is gratuitous, meaningless, and therefore absurd.

This provides a *complexio oppositorum*, a series of key tensions, which Sartre tries to work out as a tragic conflict. The Sartrean hero cannot live in a state of "nausea"; he must dedicate himself to the project he has chosen, even though he cannot justify this commitment. Why should he in his finitude struggle to fulfill himself when he is convinced of his utter insignificance in the cosmic scheme of things? The physical universe takes no cognizance of his metaphysical passion and offers him no consolations. He must transform his biological energy into a decisive choice of himself. Yet the paradox of freedom is not to be thrust aside: if life is an endless battle, that can never be won, to transform infinite possibilities into concrete actuality, what is the point of the struggle? The Sartrean protagonist must strive to make his life meaningful on a foundation of purposelessness. As André Gorz, a devout disciple of Sartre, declares in his autobiography, *The Traitor:* "He had discovered that when a man is incapable of living, or when life has no meaning for him, he always invents this way out for himself: to write about the nonmeaning of life, to look for an explanation, an escape, to demonstrate that all roads are blocked save one—this demonstration itself, and the remedy it provides against the experience it contradicts." [3]

The Existentialist is brought up short by the myth of the absurd; he must go beyond it, if he is to go anywhere at all. It is the perception of the ineradicable absurdity of existence that adds a tragic dimension to life, even as it seems to deny the possibility of creating the forms of the tragic vision. For "if nothing has any importance, then the consciousness that nothing has any importance has no importance." [4] The trap is sprung. The will to art, as Nietzsche maintained, may indeed surpass the will to truth, but the writer knows that his aesthetic devotion changes nothing in his situation. Art cannot possibly save him or his fellow men. If everything is absurd, then Existentialism too is absurd, and the Sartrean cult of freedom is as meaningless as the universe in which man, a stranger and afraid, finds himself. Absurdity is the principle that rules the universe. Absurdity is God!

Sartre's novels and plays are variations on this single theme: man is superfluous, the supernumerary of the world. The counterpoint of affirmation is brought in by showing that the "free" man knows that this is so but nevertheless goes ahead with his life. What Sartre mourns is not the death of God but the fact that life moves inexorably toward death. The Existentialist hero has infinite possibilities to choose from, but his range of freedom is cruelly curtailed by his vision of nothingness and the dread that this vision calls forth. Convulsed with doubt, burdened with a freedom which he cannot fulfill, Roquentin, in *Nausea*, perceives that the things around him are unaccountably absurd. As Sartre himself says: "Uncreated, without reason for being, without any connection with another being, being-in-itself is *de trop* for eternity." [5]

If the Existentialist hero is to exhibit any greatness of soul in his encounter with nothingness, he must judge himself, not in the light of the supernatural but in terms of what he does. Life determines the meaning of life. Action is fate. Whatever decision man makes, he cannot help but choose. The logic of Kirillov has been vindicated: "Man will be God." [6] As Sartre explicitly declares: "Existentialism is nothing else than an attempt to draw all the consequences of a coherent atheistic position. . . . Existentialism isn's so atheistic that it wears itself out showing that God doesn't exist. Rather, it declares that if God did exist, that would change nothing." [7] The hero must fight for his freedom, even though he realizes that he lives for the purpose of dying. The freedom he cherishes is actually freedom in the face of death. Existentialism calls man to take up a life of authentic striving but offers him no hope of redemption. His finitude is the test of his manhood. The sense of the absurd in a godless universe imposes a severe but not insuperable limitation on the emergence of the tragic vision.

ii

In keeping with his nihilism, Sartre's strategy of motivation derives not from individual psychology but from a kind of perspectivism which focuses on events that are in themselves incomprehensible. Hence he discards, for more or less the same reasons that dictated Kafka's and Samuel Beckett's disintegration of the formal structure of the plot, the old chronological order of narration, the framework of logical succession. Relativism reigns. Rationalism, like idealism, is overthrown. But the problem of how he is to justify his existence continues to plague the hero of *Nausea*. In the past he had spent his time chiefly in thinking of existence, sorting phenomena into conceptual pigeonholes, and then suddenly existence unveiled itself. "It had lost the harmless look of an abstract category: it was the very paste of things, this root was kneaded into existence. Or rather the root, the park gates, the bench, the sparse grass, all that had vanished: the diversity of things, their individuality, were only an appearance, a veneer." [8] The experience of "nausea," by confirming the truth of the absurd, incapacitates the hero for action. He feels that he exists and yet he cannot say what for.

The Reprieve, like *The Age of Reason*, demonstrates how difficult it is for the Sartrean hero to affirm himself. Daniel, the pederast, like the central character, Mathieu, is constantly spying upon his inner reactions, unable to accept himself as a coward and homosexual. Mathieu, the embodiment of the principle of freedom, feels that the war is no longer *his* war. "He was alone on this bridge, alone in the world, accountable to no man. 'I am free *for nothing*,' he reflected wearily. . . . And yet he must risk that freedom." [9] *Troubled Sleep*, the other novel in the trilogy, *The Roads to Freedom*, depicts the defeat of the French forces in the Second World War. Neither in battle nor in defeat can these French soldiers, walking as if in their sleep in a lurid atmosphere of despair and death, affirm their being. Mathieu looks at his comrades and thinks: "I have spent my life reading, yawning, tinkling the bell of my own little problems, I decided not to choose, only to find that I had already chosen, that I chose this war, this defeat, that today has been waiting for me since the beginning of time." [10] Yet it is obvious that these soldiers have not chosen. They have simply submitted to a vast and complex network of forces beyond their control. All they have done is to accept the meaninglessness of their fate. Even Mathieu's decision to delay the advance of the German troops and to die for nothing represents no moral victory but is a tragic affirmation of the human gift of freedom.

iii

In his dramatic work Sartre comes to close grips with the paradoxical problem of the relation of tragedy to freedom. Unlike the Greek tragic writers who took for granted a pre-existing body of moral values, Sartre insists that man confers meaning on the world. Otherwise it does not exist. Sartre recognizes no divine order to which man must subordinate himself. When he declares that the fundamental desire on the part of man is to be God, he does not mean by "God" what a Christian writer would mean. His position throughout his work is uncompromisingly antisupernaturalistic. God is an illusion, neither necessary nor justifiable. The fact of individual freedom cannot be reconciled rationally with the existence of God. And it is freedom that lies at the heart of the tragic vision. If the gods are made to play a decisive role in the resolution of the central conflict, then the freedom of the hero is placed in jeopardy. He is guilty of "bad faith." It is the element of moral freedom that makes man superior to the order of nature. God, as Orestes discovers in *The Flies*, cannot determine human reality. Nor is the world that Sartre depicts under the sway of objective, universal laws. It is contingent and meaningless. If universal determinism prevails, then there is no possibility of releasing the tragic vision.

We see how Orestes, when he gets rid of the vastly reassuring but cowardly illusion (an example of "bad faith") that he is under the special protection of the gods, experiences an exhilarating sense of freedom. He has arrived at the frightening but liberating discovery that the gods are completely powerless against those in whose heart the light of freedom shines. Once Zeus committed the blunder of bestowing on man the gift of freedom, man ceases to be a creature of the gods. Orestes becomes the savior of the city of man when he accepts the knowledge that he is entirely alone in the universe, with no one to give him orders. He will obey no other law but his own. There is no fixed "human nature." The tragic structure of *The Flies* is weakened by the heavy burden of doctrinaire dialogue it is made to carry.[11]

In *No Exit*, hell is presented as a tormenting state of perpetual awareness; the consciousness, remembering the past, maintains its endless vigil. There is no possibility of escape for these three characters shut up in one room. Garcin declares that "Alone, none of us can save himself or herself; we're linked together inextricably." [12] They are inseparable, with all eternity ahead of them. The Existentialist motif is brought out when Garcin wonders whether one can judge a life by a single action. A man, he argues, is what he wills himself to be, but Inez replies: "It's what one does, and nothing else, that shows the stuff one's made of." [13] It does not matter when one dies, how soon or late. "You are—your life, and nothing else." [14] The hell which Inez, Estelle, and Garcin inhabit gives rise to no tragic illumination. Sartre comes closest to embodying the tragic vision, in plays like *The Devil and the Good Lord* and *The Condemned of Altona*, when he deals with the universal problem of freedom as it is actually resolved in the world of men.

The Devil and the Good Lord, which takes place in the time of the Renaissance in the town of Worms, Germany, is based on the critical events that convulsed the German states during this period: the Peasants' Revolt and the Protestant Reformation. Cut off from supplies and the possibility of military help, besieged by Goetz, the ruthless conqueror, the forces trapped in Worms cannot get themselves to believe that God has deserted them. Nasti, the self-appointed prophet of revolutionary action, is resolved to incite the citizens to violence so that they will become compromised. He is willing to have them suffer misfortune, misery, devastation, and horror so that the true Kingdom of Heaven will be established on earth. That is why God needs the help of man. The Kingdom of Heaven on earth is nothing more than the community of men.

Heinrich, the priest, is faithful to the commandments of God, but even his faith is badly shaken by this terrible calamity that has befallen his people. Like Father Paneloux in *The Plague*, he must insist that nothing occurs without the express will of God, however inscrutable the action of the Lord may appear to human understanding. He regards Nasti's preachment as the vilest blasphemy. Like the crippled Kierkegaard, he cries out in torment: "**I believe because it is absurd! Absurd! Absurd!**" [15]

It is Goetz who is the hero of this Existentialist tragedy. He fears naught, neither God nor devil. He knows that he is an outcast and therefore a rebel, freely accepting his chosen destiny to be an instrument of evil. When Heinrich invokes the name of the Devil, Goetz defiantly declares that he refuses to deal with anyone but God. Though he killed his brother, God can do nothing against him. "I have committed the worst of crimes, and the God of justice is powerless to punish me." [16] The tragic vision that Sartre unfolds gets rid of the notion of divine or human justice as well as the Greek idea of retribution. Goetz will perversely go ahead with his plan of doing Evil. He has no faith in Nasti's dream of human solidarity. He does not care in the least for the welfare of mankind. A blasphemer like Ahab, he challenges God to combat. "God hears me, it is God I am deafening, and that is enough for me, for He is the only enemy worthy of my talents. . . . It is God I shall crucify this night . . . because His suffering is infinite, and renders infinite those whom He causes to suffer." [17]

Recklessly following the principle of all or nothing, Goetz turns himself into a monster. He will burn and slay, and then God will be offended and cry out that this is not what He intended at all. Like a character stepped out of the pages of *Being and Nothingness*, Goetz declares: "Yes, Lord, You are completely innocent: how can You conceive Nothing, You who are fulness itself?" [18] Goetz reaffirms the Existentialist thesis that man must assume sole responsibility for his actions. When Heinrich expounds the idea that everyone is busy perpetrating evil while doing good is impossible on earth, Goetz undergoes a sudden change of heart. He will gamble against the good Lord. If he loses, well, then the issue will be decided. He loses (by deliberately cheating) and chooses to embrace God but he is none the happier because of it. He is alone. Perhaps, he speculates sadly, God is a disaster.

Goetz desires to establish the Kingdom of God; he will set up the City of the Sun, the first truly Christian community, in this corner of the earth. But he finds that he cannot win the confidence of the peasants. When Catherine, his former mistress, who is dying, cries out for the holy priest who will give her absolution, Goetz commands God to work a miracle for him. When there is no reply, he draws the dagger from his belt, stabs the palm of his left hand, the palm of his right, and then his side. Now that he bears the stigmata on his own body, the people believe in him, but he feels all the more alone, cut off from Heaven. "Heaven is an empty hole. I even wonder where God lives." [19] The peasants listen to false prophets, like Nasti, who insist that the religion of love is born of the Devil. Goetz is filled with rage. Let the masses perish in their folly. He is now face to face with God, but what is God? Is God, he wonders, but the sweep of darkness, "the tormenting absence of everything"? [20] Goetz blesses God, nevertheless, for having revealed unto him the wickedness of men.

In his quest for the highest Good, however, Goetz is bound to suffer disillusionment. In his fanaticism he wishes to be able to distinguish the Devil from the Good Lord. But his leading motives in choosing this life of austere renunciation are suspect. His virtues are more fatal than his vices. Fundamentally he has not changed. Now he asks God: "Lord, if Thou dost refuse us the means of doing good, why hast Thou made us desire it so keenly?" [21] God remains silent. It is Heinrich who discloses the shattering truth that God remains silent because Goetz is unimportant in his eyes. Goetz knows that God gave no sign when he threw the dice; Goetz alone was responsible for the decision. He realizes at last that he is nothing in the sight of God. "God does not see me, God does not hear me, God does not know me. . . . Silence is God. Absence is God. God is the loneliness of man. There was no one but myself; I alone decided on Evil; and I alone invented Good. It was I who cheated, I who worked miracles, I who accused myself today, I alone who can absolve myself; I, man. If God exists, man is nothing." [22] This is the revelation of the truth that God does not exist.

This is "the nausea" of nothingness to which Heinrich, the apostate priest, cannot reconcile himself. When in his fury he tries to choke Goetz, the latter stabs him to death with the cry: "The comedy of Good has ended with a murder." [23] As night falls, Goetz knows of a certainty that God is dead. He no longer needs God. It is foolish, he concludes, to attempt to do good on earth; good and evil are inseparable. He agrees to commit evil in order to become good. As leader of the peasant army, he will tell his followers that God is dead. He killed God because God had separated him from the body of mankind. He takes command of the army with the proclamation: "The kingdom of man is beginning." [24] Alone, under an empty sky, he will fight for the vindication of a truth not to be endured. His triumph lies in his willingness to face his lonely destiny and bear the burden of cosmic despair.

The Condemned of Altona is a tragedy of our time that searches out the problem of guilt in the heart of man. Unlike *The Flies* or *The Devil and the Good Lord*, it is relatively free of Existentialist doctrine. The Von Gerlach shipbuilding company in Altona, a suburb of Hamburg, represents a dynasty that considers itself safe whatever the group in Germany that occupies the seat of power. The father, a patriarchal figure of immense authority, is now but a figurehead in a huge corporation. Knowing that he is doomed to die of cancer in the space of six months, he gathers his family about him in order to make clear how affairs are to be managed after his death.

There is a skeleton in the family closet. The older son Franz is not dead, as reported, but lives hidden upstairs in the family mansion, refusing to see anyone but his sister, who brings him food and lives with him incestuously. In the past he helped a Polish rabbi who had fled from the concentration camp the Nazis had built on land they bought from old Von Gerlach. When this was discovered, the rabbi was seized and Franz, as a punishment, was forced to witness his murder. As we learn in a series of flashbacks, Franz fought in the German army on the Russian front. His display of courage was but an outward seeming; inwardly he was pursued by the furies of guilt. In a moment of crisis, he, too, had ordered Russian partisans to be murdered. Now, hidden upstairs, he nurses the delusion that Germany has been reduced to rubble. That is how he appeases his sense of personal guilt. If Germany were prostrate and in ruins, this would constitute punishment for her crimes, whereas if he knew she were prospering he would have no justification for his self-imposed martyrdom.

His neurosis gradually disappears. He enters once more the world of time and recognizes the nature of the lie he had deliberately nurtured. He had fled from the truth of reality. He refuses to be saved. "All roads are closed; there isn't even the choice of a lesser evil." [25] In the last act, in a scene reminiscent of *The Brothers Karamazov*, Franz says: "There isn't a God, is there?" and the father replies: "I'm afraid not. It's rather a nuisance at times." [26] After the suicide of father and son has taken place, Leni, the sister, decides to occupy Franz's room and assume his burden of guilt. At the very end the tape recorder emits Franz's voice: "Perhaps there will be no more centuries after ours. Perhaps a bomb will blow out all the lights. Everything will be dead—eyes, judges, time." [27]

Existentialist tragedy heightens but does not surrender to the absurd irony of the human situation. Everything in the human condition remains problematical and contingent. In his quest of freedom, the Existentialist hero is doomed to failure, but it is this fact of failure that justifies his struggle. There are no absolutes. He must set up his own goals of striving and endow these with value in the world of men in which he fulfills himself or not at all. No external power can guarantee that the undertaking to which he gives himself is intrinsically good. This means, as Simone de Beauvoir points out, that "man, in his vain attempt to *be* God, makes himself exist *as* man." [28] The sterile question whether life is worth living must be abandoned. The principle of tragic affirmation that Existentialism dialectically brings into play is, briefly, as follows: Man is a nothing in relation to the universe; hence it is up to him to transform death into life, the contingent into the necessary, the meaningless into the meaningful.

This is the nihilism *in extremis* out of which the tragic vision is shaped.

Sartre captures the paradoxical secret of the tragic affirmation when he emphasizes that man must make his own world even as he realizes that this order imposed by the human will is not necessary. Since there are no categorical imperatives except those that man himself chooses and obeys, the Sartrean hero is not the victim of universal determinism. He cannot excuse the actions of his past; what he did was of his own making. He cannot justify what happened in terms of fate or God or the libido or economic circumstances. He makes his own free choice, without hope of ultimate justification. By accepting this hard condition, by living dangerously, Sartre's tragic heroes save themselves from falling into "bad faith."

Sartre declares that Existentialism for the first time makes human life possible. Sartre's tragic humanism rests on an atheistic premise. Since God does not exist, man must give up the futile search for standards outside himself. There is nothing disheartening in the discovery that man is alone in the universe. Man, the being who cannot be defined, begins as a nothing and then takes upon himself the task of making himself what he wishes to become. The dialectic of opposites that supports Sartre's philosophy of the tragic is at a loss when it seeks to demonstrate, in imaginative rather than ideological terms, what man is to do with his freedom. Goetz knew that all values are humanly created, but this renders every commitment suspect. The Existentialist hero is inwardly a battleground of contradictions, and yet he must believe in himself and act out the absurd grandeur of his destiny without justification. The tragic vision emerges in twentieth-century literature when it rises above its nihilistic assumptions, without repudiating them. Sartre, as in *The Flies* and *The Devil and the Good Lord*, struggled to create a type of tragedy which reveals the greatness as well as the nothingness of man.

10 TRAGEDY AND THE MARXIST SYNTHESIS

LIKE THE Christian promise of salvation in the other world, Marxist eschatology is fundamentally opposed to the tragic outlook, though for strategically different reasons. Optimistic in its envisagement of the historical future, it assures "the true believer" that the millenial dream will be fulfilled: the establishment of the Kingdom of Heaven on earth. Defeat is not ultimate. Justice will finally prevail in the dialectical process of history. Nature is rational in structure and therefore controllable by the power of reason. Hence the demand in Soviet Russia for "optimistic" drama, which affirms the triumph of man over necessity. To indulge in tragedy is, in the Communist state, a species of treason, a counter-revolutionary act. But Marxist ideology is hamstrung by its own logic: to compose tragedies that are "optimistic" in tone and content is a contradiction in terms.

For the sake of bringing about the ideal commonwealth founded on equality, justice, and "authentic" freedom, the dedicated Communist must surrender what is, after all, only a bourgeois illusion: the myth of individuality. Sloughing off the fractious, separate self, he must be prepared to sacrifice everything for the sake of the collectivity, which is immortal. The sacrifice the revolutionary martyr makes for the sake of a "higher" cause is rewarded at the end, even if he perishes in the struggle. History is on the side of the embattled proletariat. The ideal of the classless society is bound to triumph. The Marxist dialectic usurps the role of the *deus ex machina*. By throwing off the trammels of a false morality imposed by the ruling class, the militant Communist discovers the law of necessity and thus inherits his birthright of freedom.

Economics thus becomes the all-powerful principle of destiny. Necessity rules, though the individual is endowed with the freedom, based on a scientific knowledge of the processes of social and physical causation, to support the proletariat in its efforts to cast off the age-old bondage of class exploitation. Once this is achieved and the classless society inaugurated, man will be king over himself, no longer subject to the blind dictates of mechanical forces. His individual will, no longer thwarted, will be harmoniously merged in the collective will. Inflexibly rational in its *Weltanschauung*, Marxism strips aside the snarled, factitious bundle of motives supposed to govern human behavior: the pull of the unconscious, the influence of the irrational, the spiritual element, the romantic quest for transcendence. The pressure of economics is the mother of morality. The system of production determines the prevailing complex of right and wrong, good and evil, justice and injustice.

As we shall try to show, dialectical materialism, with its crude Pavlovian conception of human nature, spells the death of the tragic vision. The hero who is denied the existential illusion, if illusion it be, of free choice, is prevented from participating in any tragic conflict. The outcome is assured in advance. Determinism in human behavior discounts the element of the human will. The Marxist seeks, of course, to demonstrate that consciousness does play a part in the shaping of history, that individual wills with their purposive striving do produce a calculable effect in the course of the revolutionary struggle. On the other hand, it is equally important to show that, despite temporary setbacks, the economic laws do ultimately assert themselves. The victory of the proletariat is guaranteed not by any mystical fiat but by the inexorable determinism of events.[1]

Hence when Marxist critics turn their attention to

literature, which is only a part of the cultural superstructure, they would put an end to all forms of romantic
idealism, the bourgeois apotheosis of love, the metaphysical fetishism of absolute truth, and particularly the reprehensible notion that literature has no organic relation to
subject matter. Not that the writer presents his ideas
baldly like a journalist, but the ideological foundation on
which his work rests is considered to be of the highest
importance in assessing its merit. Those writers who concern themselves solely with form "always reveal a hopeless
and negative attitude to their social environment." [2] This
denunciation of "negativism" carries over into the twentieth century; it is evident in the critical evaluation of
Soviet literature produced during the thaw, from 1954 to
1957.[3] Judging literature exclusively in terms of content,
that is, in terms of ideas, the Marxist critics consistently
intellectualized the work of art.

But, as we have seen, "positive" or "optimistic" ideas
do not belong within a tragic context. The tragic writers
deal not with such abstractions as class consciousness or
revolutionary imperatives but with the irreducible complexities of human nature, always individualized and in
the last analysis mysterious. The conflicts of the tragic
hero, modern or ancient, are never "determined" by economic forces alone. He chooses to act and his choice,
whatever its underlying pattern of motivation, represents
a free thrust of the will. In taking action, Orestes, in
Sartre's play, changes himself and transforms the character
of the social order. The revolutionary terrorist may, like
Kaliayev in The Just Assassins, decide to hurl the bomb
which will kill the Archduke, but the decision is his own:
a deliberate "crime" for which he is willing to pay with
his life. As Malraux makes clear in Man's Fate, no two
members of a class or the Party react inwardly in the
same manner, even though they may both carry out orders
issued from above. Concerned with human nature in the
abstract and particularly with the task of revolutionary
"engineering," Marxism drastically minimizes the role of
the individual. An ethic of Promethean defiance based

on the assumption that the forces which govern the universe can be brought under human control by scientific means, Marxism rejects the world of "spirit" which the tragic vision seeks to explore.

ii

In the Marxist version of man in relation to society, the individual is thus steadily pushed into the background. All ideals, social in both origin and effect, are relative in time and place. There are no moral absolutes. Man creates his own standards of what he considers desirable. (Much of this is also basic to Sartrean Existentialism.) The Marxist man has gone beyond the need for tragedy. The tragic sense of life is a superstitious relic of a time when men were demoralized by a morbid fear of death. That is how Marxist ideology disposes of the conflicts which culminate in the tragic vision: the *Angst* of human existence, the sickness unto death that Kierkegaard described, the demonic struggle of an Ivan Karamazov or a Stavrogin, the nihilistic torments of a Nietzsche, the dread of the vision of Nothingness that Heidegger analyzes, the problematical relationship of man to the Absolute that Sartre dramatizes in *The Devil and the Good Lord*. Everything under the sun is reduced to a single economic necessity. According to the Marxist world-view, progress is real; history is on the side of the revolutionary cause. As Joseph Needham prophetically announces: "The Kingdom of God is no unearthly conceptual realm, but a just and happy social order." [4] By accepting the limitations imposed by necessity, man can bring the tragedy of existence to an end. But the conception of the tragic vision that we have set forth is born precisely of man's struggle to achieve the impossible, to conquer the fatality of time and rise above the body of this death, to transcend the finite and the given, to impose order and unity of meaning on a universe that defeats his aspirations and renders absurd his ambition to become like unto God.

In the Marxist system of aesthetics, tragedy is viewed, like all of literature and art, as a social product. George

Thomson sets out to interpret the history of Greek tragedy, particularly the work of Aeschylus, in relation to the
psychological repercussions of the class conflict in Athens.
For example, Ananke, or Necessity, "represents the principle that the laboring members of society are denied all
share in the products of their labour beyond the mini-
mum necessary to keep them labouring." [5] A critic like
Christopher Caudwell points out that "bourgeois" poetry
perpetuates the pernicious illusion of individual freedom,
so that the bourgeois can see himself "as an heroic figure
fighting a lone fight for freedom." [6] Proletarian art, on
the other hand, seeks to become coincident with society.
To the wavering bourgeois writer, Caudwell has the militant proletariat address this message:

> There is no neutral world of art, free from categories or
> determining causes. Art is a social activity. . . . You must
> choose between class art which is unconscious of its cau-
> sality and is therefore to that extent false and unfree, and
> proletarian art which is becoming conscious of its causality
> and will therefore emerge as the truly free art of com-
> munism. There is no classless art except communist art,
> and that is not yet born; and class art today, unless it is
> proletarian, can only be the art of a dying class. [7]

Despite this declaration of faith in the messianic future,
the fact remains that Soviet Russia has effectually "liquidated" the literature of the tragic vision, while it is a dying
class which has fathered the work of such men as O'Neill,
Strindberg, Malraux, Faulkner, Camus, and Sartre.

The Soviet hero embodies a new breed of man: he is
the proletarian savior, the revolutionary committed to the
mystique of action. Sustained by a scientific concept of
reality, he is animated by a large hope, a constructive ideology of revolt. It was this rationalistic, optimistic hero,
whose portrait is drawn in Chernyshevsky's *What Is to
Be Done?*, whom Dostoevski castigated. In effect, Cher-
nyshevski would banish tragedy altogether by challenging
the Greek concept of fate. "The tragic has no essential
connection with the idea of fate or necessity. In real life
the tragic is most often adventitious, it does not spring

from the essence of preceding events." [8] The Russian realists categorically demanded that the writer must show life
as it is and how it should be.[9] There is the force of the
ethical injunction: what *should be must be*. "Thus, tragedy, in any form, is challenged at its very foundation by
the optimism of the dialectic." [10]

Officially the Marxist theoreticians insisted that literature as a revolutionary weapon must be optimistic and
affirmative, but a number of critics continued to concern
themselves with the aim of helping to create a representative type of Soviet "tragedy." This presented a difficult
problem in aesthetic casuistry. For tragedy obviously had
no place in a land which had liberated the proletariat and
conferred on man the freedom which would enable him
to govern his own fate. The Aristotelian theory of catharsis would have to go. Tragedy should not call forth pity
or terror. Instead, it should arouse the dynamic force of
inspiration, combined with an element of pity for those
who are still the victims of economic oppression. The
revolutionary hero may be overcome in his struggle—
inwardly, of course, he remains unconquered—but his
martyrdom should function to energize the collective will
of the masses. But if his cause lives on and is destined to
triumph, there is, there can be, no tragic resolution.

Bertold Brecht, the social realist who is eager to hasten
the redemption of humanity from the curse of economic
bondage, takes up such themes as degeneracy, perversion,
crime, murder, rape, prostitution, alcoholism, and war.
Here is a gifted dramatist who, in denouncing the dehumanized system of capitalism, invokes the myth of the
class war, producing plays charged with revolutionary fervor and replete with propagandistic slogans. The motif of
the class war, in his later work, is always present behind
the *mise en scène*. The theater is employed principally as
a means of enlightenment in order to transform the structure of society. The clue to Brecht's dramaturgy is to be
found in his conviction that man must not regard himself
as the predestined victim of forces beyond his control.

In a note to *Antigone*, Brecht declares: "Man's fate is

himself." [11] O'Neill also voiced this belief, but the emphasis in Brecht's work is differently placed. As a writer of
epic dramas that concentrate on social problems, Brecht
deliberately eschews the tragic vision. His dramatic docu-
mentaries furnish a simplified version of reality. The rich,
as in *The Caucasian Chalk Circle*, are evil while the poor
are exemplars of virtue. Didactic in tone, his plays are
addressed to the intellect; they are designed to awaken
critical awareness in the audience. In his non-Aristotelian
dramas, the hero is not doomed by the iron hand of fate;
he is the conscious agent of a revolutionary purpose.
Brecht reveals the pain and suffering endured by those
who have not yet reached the millenium of the classless
state, but he is not writing tragedy.

Brecht pictures a world that is filled with cruelty and
competitive hatred; pain is inflicted, pain is endured. It
is a horribly grotesque world, and what makes it all the
more grotesque is that a remedy is available for this condition. The humanity of man is crushed out of him not
by the hostility of the universe but by the absurd contradictions and inequities of capitalist society. People suffer
bitterly but they fail to comprehend the cause of their
suffering; they attribute it to fate or the malignity of the
universe or the human condition, whereas in reality it
springs from the diseased civilization they live in. Brecht,
it is true, did not create "the positive" hero according to
the ideological prescriptions of socialist realism. The protagonist in *Mother Courage*, a memorable symbolic figure
of endurance in the midst of war, is portrayed with earthy
irony. Though Brecht exposed the cruel waste and horror
of life in the modern world, he was writing comedy, not
tragedy. Eric Bentley writes, by way of defence: "However
anti-tragic a poet's philosophy, if he is truly a poet, the
tragedy of his life will find some echoes in his work." [12]
The incidental echoes are present in Brecht's work, but
such a loose formulation of the meaning of the tragic
vision serves to abolish all distinctions.

The Marxist aesthetic, because it is ruled by the prag-
matic assumption that happiness for man is attainable,
negates the tragic vision. Once the problem of economic

security for all is solved, then all other problems will be automatically taken care of. It is economic misery, in short, that is the root-cause of metaphysical despair and world-weariness. The tragic view rejects the belief in happiness to be achieved through economic planning or revolutionary transformations. Gottfried Benn, the nihilist, was appalled by the Marxist aesthetic, applied ruthlessly on the Soviet scene during the thirties, which results in the total elimination of the inner life, the drama of the mind. Benn asks the crucial question: "Is man, in the last analysis of his essence, rooted in a naturalistic, materialistic, economic condition, determined in his structure by hunger and clothes?" [13] Benn deplores all formal attempts to organize life as if it were a problem in technological efficiency. The nature of man is not fundamentally changed by improvements in the technique of getting his food and producing material goods. Benn declares "that in all economic systems man remains the tragic being, the divided ego, whose abysses cannot be filled with bread and woolen vests, whose dissonances cannot be dissolved in the rhythms of the *Internationale*." [14] Suffering cannot be eradicated by gadgets, bread, and circuses. Those who strive to reconstruct life according to some Socialist blueprint are hastening the death of art. It is fatal for the artist to succumb to the ideologies of his age, to dabble in theories and abstractions. What must be recovered and reaffirmed is the tragic man.

Tragic man transcends his occupational or class role. The tragic vision, which rests on a metaphysical foundation, extends far beyond the age or place in which it manifests itself. It offers no final answers, no constructive solutions. Dostoevski, who belongs prophetically to our time, reveals in *The Possessed* the horrifying consequences of an ideology which refuses to acknowledge the tragic sense of life.

iii

Dostoevski, in *The Possessed*, one of the best political novels ever written, does not neglect the forces of opposition in his imaginative analysis of the political

struggle. Although he was himself a devout religious believer, he portrayed with profound psychological insight
the character of the fanatical revolutionary and the reasons why he succumbs to the dangerous temptations of an
abstract and inhuman ideology. Dostoevski knew inti-
mately the spellbinding power of the evangel of radical-
ism. Though he had given up his faith in political
messianism, he never, as an artist, sweated it completely
out of his system. A man of passionate extremes, he found
conservatism alien to his way of thought. As Irving Howe
notes: "Behind his radical Christianity and his mystic
populism there is always a sense of being one with the
insulted and the injured." [15]

He understood what "possession" meant, be it political
or religious or diabolical in nature. With unfailing compassion he diagnoses the disease of nihilism from which
Stavrogin suffers, his inability to feel and, worse, his
incapacity to act upon his feelings. A badly split personality, he is the man who, all passion spent, stands apart
from life. He is the literary father of a whole brood of
metaphysical rebels who crowd the twentieth-century
scene. Like Meursault and Caligula, he has thrown off
the restraints of morality, though at heart he continues to
search for an ultimate solution, but without hope that he
will ever achieve it. Camus, who dramatized *The Possessed*, regards it as a prophetic novel in that it introduced
protagonists who cannot give themselves in love, "wanting
to believe and yet unable to do so—like those who people
our society and our spiritual world today." [16] In short, it is
a contemporary work he is dramatizing.

Though *The Possessed* reveals the degree to which
ideology can tyrannize over the minds of men so that they
become the victims of the mechanical abstractions they
themselves have fathered, Dostoevski does not set forth a
counter-ideology. He depicts without distortion a set of
characters who serve the cause of the revolution, men
whose conscience is so perverted that they reject all bonds
of human solidarity. Just as in *The Brothers Karamazov*
he does not tip the balance in favor of Alyosha or Father

Zossima, so in this tragic novel he identifies himself with all his characters. He is not guilty of simplifying, and therefore falsifying, the complex body of motives that govern the actions, however absurd or outrageously queer, of his *dramatis personae*.

Stavrogin is one of "the possessed." Then there is Pyotr Stepanovitch Verhovensky, a revolutionist, active behind the scenes. Stavrogin occupies the center of the stage. Shigalov, the personification of all that is unconscionably cruel in the mind and heart of the revolutionary extremist, carries the logic of the myth of violence to absurd lengths. Shatov, a serf by birth, suspects that these revolutionary conspirators are motivated fundamentally by a destructive feeling of hatred. If Russia were to be reformed and its flagrant abuses eliminated, they would be rendered terribly unhappy. Whom would they then have to hate?

The novel highlights the folly of these revolutionary agitators, their vanity, their lack of courage, the ambivalent motives that sway them, their willingness to commit murder. Stavrogin has come to warn Shatov that he is in danger of being killed by the revolutionists. Shatov had joined the group before he went off to America but there changed his mind and sought to resign. He was requested to take charge of a clandestine printing press, and he agreed in the hope that this would be his last assignment. The revolutionary group, however, has no intention of letting him go, even though he insists on his right to break away. The plan is to dispose of him on the ground that he is a spy. Stavrogin understands the true character of Verhovensky, who is behind the plot: he is a madman. Pyotr feels an immeasurable contempt for these deluded provincial revolutionaries, whose vanity he exploits to the limit. Stavrogin quietly suggests that an excellent motive for binding them together is to persuade them to become accomplices in a murder; then they would be Pyotr's slaves for life.

Shigalov, the gloomy reformer, has worked out a method for reorganizing society on logical lines, though he is compelled to admit that his system is not yet complete.

"Starting from unlimited freedom, I arrive at unlimited despotism." [17] He is reduced to despair by this syllogistic contretemps: in the ideal state of the future one-tenth of the population enjoys absolute liberty and absolute power while the others must practice the strict virtue of obedience. Pyotr outlines the short cut to the revolution which will bestow freedom on humanity and liberate it from the oppression of the past. The way to this blessed consummation lies through murder.

Dostoevski is not drawing a malicious caricature of these "free-thinking" revolutionaries with their proclaimed policy of universal destruction. As a tragic writer he brings sharply into focus the dilemma of the Communist man, the rational man, who has overthrown the absolute of religion and replaced it with the absolutism of power. If there is no supreme moral obligation, then the end justifies the means, even if this ethic of expediency culminates in political murder. Dostoevski's creative purpose is to show that the denial of God was bound to lead the revolutionary conspirators inevitably into crime.

In the name of an abstract ideal of equality, these revolutionists dogmatically deny the tragic ambiguity of the human condition. Shigalov, for example, has worked out a system of spying, which uncannily anticipates some of the totalitarian controls Orwell describes in *Nineteen Eighty-Four*. "Every member of the society spies on the others, and it's his duty to inform against them. Every one belongs to all and all to every one. All are slaves and equal in their slavery." [18] In extreme cases Shigalov advocates slander and lies and even murder, but he still maintains that the supreme ideal is equality. Pyotr explains the nature of Shigalovism. Great men "will be banished and put to death. Cicero will have his tongue cut out, Copernicus will have his eyes put out, Shakespeare will be stoned—that's Shigalovism. Slaves are bound to be equal. There has never been either freedom or equality without despotism, but in the herd there is bound to be equality, and that's Shigalovism!" [19] The tragic element in life can be conquered. Culture and art can be proscribed. The great need in the world is the imposition of discipline. The thirst for culture, Pyotr declares, "is an aristocratic thirst." Every genius will be stifled in its infancy. "We'll reduce all to a common denominator! Complete equality!" [20]

This is the brave new world Pyotr would establish by putting the master plan of Shigalovism into operation. The new race of slaves, their individuality totally crushed, will be free from the pull of desire. Corrupted by vodka and vice, they will no longer regard crime as reprehensible. Russia will be plunged in darkness. Shatov, who by this time has broken irrevocably with the enemies of freedom, declares that all the revolutionists have to offer is "a glorious mediocrity of the most bourgeois kind, contemptible shallowness, a jealous equality, equality without individual dignity." [21]

That is how Dostoevski comes to grips with the tragic implications of the revolutionary theme. Stavrogin, the nihilistic hero, a man devoid of hope, has ceased to believe that his life can be redeemed. He cannot share the political dreams of the revolutionaries. He can never give himself wholly to an idea like Kirillov or Shatov. Even the act of killing himself he knows will be another sham, "the last deception in an endless series of deceptions," [22] the final act of absurdity. The utopian vision of the classless society ends in a fiasco of blood, destruction, and betrayal.

iv

What is distinctive in Dostoevski's handling of the political theme in *The Possessed* is that he reduces the abracadabra of ideological abstractions to human terms and situates the central conflict in the heart of his principal characters. They are in search of an existential meaning, a life-purpose, a sustaining faith. He shows to what lengths they are prepared to go in pursuit of their revolutionary aims. The deification of reason leads to Shigalovism: freedom is transformed in topsy-turvy fashion into slavery, truth into falsehood, the cult of equality into oppression. Stavrogin cannot reconcile himself to such a perversion of values, and he returns home and hangs himself. For Dostoevski the only "logical" end left open for the nihilist is suicide.

Camus, like Dostoevski, is not deluded by purely political or economic panaceas. Like Shigalov, the fanatical Communist allows ideology to take the place of humane values and therefore turns politics into an immoral technique of seizing power. Having gone beyond nihilism, Camus supports a *metaphysical* revolt which affirms the fundamental need of human solidarity. Man, not the Marxist dialectic, is the measure of all things. Camus carries Dostoevski's logic one step further. No demented visionary like Kirillov, he spells out the consequences of godlessness in the modern world. Man, prisoner of time, becomes God himself.

Camus is not blind to the dangers attendant upon such a radical transvaluation of values. If man takes upon himself the burden of freedom, he can satiate his irrepressible lust for power without being held back by any sense of conscience. Moral nihilism is thus transformed into a deadly will to power. Alone in the universe, with nothing to restrain his instinct of aggression, the man-God commits crimes in behalf of a dehumanized reason. He acts confidently on the premise that he can find fulfillment in the domain of history. Revolution, which seeks to impose world unity by force, is given over to abstract principles and condones the ethics of murder. Ideology unchecked by any moral code becomes irresponsible and degenerates into a defence of totalitarianism. Once the nihilistic revolution is unleashed, the career of appalling crime starts on its course. The final judgment will come at the end of time, when history will present its account. Hence every revolutionary action which succeeds, whatever the cost in human suffering and bloodshed, is justified. The Revolution as the supreme goal of striving transcends the bond of brotherhood and the claims of love.

The Russian terrorists, as Camus shows in *The Just Assassins*, died for an unknown future. They felt that life was sacred and yet they gallantly sacrificed their own life. Though they resorted to violence, they nevertheless possessed this redeeming trait: they were willing to pay for their acts with their own life. But after 1905 the myth of innocence is abandoned. Nihilism triumphs. Power is the single end sought. Unlike Sartre, Camus contends that the true rebel, instead of accepting the Communist incitement to violence, turns against the Revolution. Otherwise he falls into lamentable contradiction. "Every revolutionary ends by becoming either an oppressor or a heretic." [23] Only as a heretic can he be a tragic figure involved in a tragic conflict. The ethics of rebellion, unlike the ethical commands of Communism, is at least conformable to the tragic outlook, since it recognizes the responsibility of the individual. It affirms a human nature common to all men and refuses to treat man as a thing. Unlike the revolutionary, the rebel does not work in terms of absolutes, however dialectically conceived, and in this way justify whatever evils and abominations are committed in his time. He will not sacrifice others, only himself.

It is by concentrating attention on the moral responsibility of the politically committed hero that Camus restores the possibility of achieving the tragic vision. *The State of Siege*, which is constructed like a morality play, describes the fearful struggle man must wage for the priceless gift of freedom, the blow he must have the courage to strike against all the forces that seek to terrorize and enslave mankind. As in *The Plague*, it is the visitation of death that instills ghastly fear into the populace and prevents them from affirming their humanity. Nada, who is doing his duty under the new totalitarian regime, gleefully wishes to destroy everything. The age of the concentration camp and crematoria has supervened. The people are panic-stricken, afraid to speak out in protest. As in Tennessee Williams' *Camino Real*, the authorities outlaw the emotion of love, the ties of brotherhood.

Diego, the protagonist, refuses to escape from the plague-infested city when the opportunity presents itself. Overcoming his fear, he breaks out in revolt against "the system." The chorus utters a great cry of rejoicing. His message of liberation is simple but inspiring: the people must protest against the destiny of death. When they abandon despair and, like men, embrace their freedom, the rains begin to fall on the parched earth. Like Orestes in *The Flies*, Diego will not accept a form of justice that brings harm to others. He rejects the logic of Shigalovism: "To do away with murder we must kill, and to prevent injustice we must do violence." [24] No one must be entrusted with absolute power. That is how the Plague, personified symbol of tyranny, is vanquished. There are limits beyond which man must not attempt to go.

The State of Siege is too abstract in developing its central theme; its presentation of allegorically intended characters prevents the play from becoming an effective example of the tragic vision. It is, nevertheless, a vigorous defence of the individual, a moving vindication of the human "against the abstractions and terrors of the totalitarian state, whether Russian, German, or Spanish." [25] It is the bureaucratic state, absolutist in power and repressive in function, which Camus singles out as the evil that must be abolished. Freedom must always be protected.

A more profound tragedy of sacrifice in the revolutionary cause is given in *The Just Assassins*. Basing his play on an historical episode, Camus reveals the peculiar temptations that face the revolutionary: the doubts that assail his inner faith, the fears that undermine his courage to kill, his love of life that makes death a cruel deprivation. Camus, in this play, tries to make clear that violence has limits which no man, however sincere his devotion to the revolutionary cause, must transgress. If one does go beyond them, as Kaliayev does, then he must be prepared to pay for the crime with the loss of his own life.

The terrorists in Moscow in 1905 are plotting to assassinate the Grand Duke Serge, their aim being to free the downtrodden masses from intolerable oppression. Kaliayev, a poet enchanted by the beauty of the world, has been chosen to hurl the bomb. He believes that the revolution must be fought for the sake of life, not for the sake of vengeful destruction. The conspirators must kill in order to create a new world in which innocence will inherit the earth. To die for a worthy humanist cause—that is the only justification for terrorism. Kaliayev refuses to accept the reasoning of a fanatical revolutionary like Stepan, who insists that everything is permissible. The sacrifice of a few lives matters very little when weighed in the balance against the misery of millions. Kaliayev, however, will kill only in the name of justice. He will not sacrifice everything for a problematical future that he will never be alive to witness. "I refuse," he declares heretically, "to add to the living injustices all around me for the sake of a dead justice." [26]

In prison, after he has carried out the deed, he spurns the bribe of life if he will betray his comrades. He committed no crime, only an act of justice. Having passed judgment on himself he is willing to meet his own death, knowing that it will be a glorious one. Camus depicts the struggle not in terms of abstract economic forces dialectically working out their own predestined pattern in the arena of history; the struggle takes place in the heart of the tragic hero who is about to throw the bomb, the man in prison who is determined to atone with his life for the necessary "crime" he committed. It is not the ideologist who carries out the deed. It is the tragic hero with his passionate love of life and his haunting sense of responsibility for himself and all who will live after him—it is he who hurls the bomb and consents to his own death.

WHEREAS Marxist ideology is fundamentally antitragic,
Sartre's Existentialism leaves room for the expression of
the tragic vision. This is not intended to imply that the
theme of revolutionary politics cannot be treated tragi-
cally. Sartre does justice to the theme in *The Devil and
the Good Lord* and *Dirty Hands*, Camus in *The Just Assassins*. *Darkness at Noon* and *Man's Fate* both embody
the tragic vision. But in each of these works the tragic
hero is no mere Party man, no "positive" figure, fanati-
cally loyal to abstract ideological principles, blindly con-
formist. Sartre's protagonist, though a Communist, is a
free agent, responsible for his decisions; he is the conscious architect of history, though he can never be sure
that the future will justify the sacrifices he is making in
the present. Sartre, like Camus, protests against a political absolutism that would sacrifice lives for the sake of the
State or the dream of the classless society to be achieved
ages hence. In conformity with his tragic humanism,
Sartre opposes the concept of class consciousness, whether
bourgeois or capitalist or proletarian in nature. Such a
categorization would exclude the element of subjectivity
and freedom that plays so important a role in Sartre's ontology. Though ideology grows out of the dynamics of the
class struggle, Sartre knows that even in a so-called classless society conflicts would still go on.

Despite his leftist leanings, Sartre has consistently criti-
cized those ideologies of our time that fail to allow room
for the affirmation of individual freedom. Freedom—that

is the dominant theme of his Existentialist plays and novels. The authentic individual acts as if he were free, exempt from environmental determination, and actually he is free. Freedom is inherent in the human condition, but man must struggle to achieve it. His freedom cannot be forced upon the procrustean bed of any political ideology. The end does not justify the means. The individual devotes himself to a deliberately chosen social ideal, but he is necessarily limited in time and effectiveness. The actions he initiates have unpredictable consequences. Despite all the planning men do, the historical process remains ambiguous. It is this Existentialist sense of the tragic in history that runs counter to the indwelling optimism of Marxist ideology. Sartre discloses a world that remains irreducibly absurd. It is man with his human subjectivity who imposes value on the world of things. Human life is purposive while the world of things is devoid of meaning.

In his plays Sartre shows how man opposes the myth of the absurd by dedicating himself to his freely chosen projects, but the absurdity is not thereby overcome. No system of values can be justified by reference to a "natural" order. The absurdity of the universe cannot be denied without undermining the responsibility of the tragic hero. He must act, even though the world in which he has his being remains not only alien but hostile. The freedom he inherits is a constant source of suffering, since he must forever strive to reach a goal of self-realization which is beyond attainment.

It is not surprising to find that Marxists stigmatize the literature of Existentialism as defeatist and decadent, a faithful reflection of the pessimism that infects the dying body of Western culture. Sartre is guilty of rejecting one of the decisive features of Marxism: the philosophy of economic determinism. It is the Existentialist exaltation of man as the bearer of freedom that the Marxists dismiss as a species of bourgeois mystification. The Sartrean hero is neither proletarian nor bourgeois but a lonely individual struggling to lead an authentic existence. Characters like

Goetz, Roquentin, Mathieu, and Hugo are denounced as prime examples of aberrant individualism and diseased subjectivity. One English critic condemns Existentialism as "an ideological weapon against the whole struggle for social betterment. Existentialism, at any rate in its classical form, resists all collective social action." [1] The Existentialist hero is a monad, alienated from nature and society, who repudiates the doctrine of economic determinism. It is this very repudiation, however, that insures his freedom of action and turns him into a tragic figure.

Communist literary spokesmen detect in this perverse insistence on the freedom of the individual the metaphysical defence of a rootless nihilism. Existentialist man, overcome by the meaninglessness of existence, realizes his total isolation from mankind. His obsession with the myth of nothingness symbolizes his loss of faith in life. Georg Lukacz roundly declares: "The nothingness which fascinates recent philosophers is a myth of declining capitalist society." [2] Such a sweeping negative judgment utterly misses the point of the paradox: the obsessed awareness of death on the part of the Existentialist hero only serves to intensify his hunger for life. Indeed, Existentialism is informed with a positive content, without ever losing sight of the tragic condition in which man is involved; it embodies man's perennial quest for freedom. Sartre pictures a world of freedom and possibility in which human choices decide the character of the future. Existentialism does not castrate man, as Roger Garaudy angrily charges, nor does it lead to "reactionary" conclusions.[3] It simply strives to tell the whole truth about the life of man.

Dirty Hands deals with the difficulties the intellectual faces when he endeavors to take up the life of political action. Like Camus in *The Just Assassins*, Sartre contrasts the hard, disciplined Communist with the soft, introspective intellectual who is never sure that he is real or that his choices are the right ones or that his feelings for others are genuine. Hugo, the intellectual, is addicted to the Existentialist "vice" of self-analysis, scrupulously examining every motive for the action he has been assigned to carry out until he is no longer able to act. While in prison he had brooded a great deal, re-enacting in his imagination the murder he had committed, trying to discover the motives that actually prompted his pulling of the trigger. He knows that the Party now wants to get rid of him; he is no longer useful. It is impossible, he argues with himself, to do exactly what the Party commands. Had he not shot Hoederer according to orders? This, as it turns out, is far from the truth.

The comrades wish to liquidate Hugo when he is released from prison, but Olga begs them to give him another chance. Perhaps he can still be redeemed. What counts heavily against him in the eyes of the professional revolutionaries is that he is a bourgeois individualist, governed by impulse, not amenable to discipline. Why did he finally shoot Hoederer? Was he motivated by jealous passion or revolutionary zeal? The play goes back two years in time. A violent factional dispute is raging within the Party, and Hugo announces that he is prepared to dispose of Hoederer, who is "objectively" an ideological traitor. He must be put out of the way for the sake of maintaining Party unity.

As secretary to Hoederer, he tries to convince his superior that he is not an impotent intellectual, but he continues to procrastinate. Everything appears to him as a game of make-believe. His wife Jessica realizes that he is incapable of performing the deed. Hugo tries hard to put his tainted bourgeois past behind him but he still reads poetry—a decidedly "negative" trait in a revolutionary conspirator. His mind is plagued with too many disturbing questions. He is at war with himself, forever seeking to find out if he is right in wanting what he thinks he wants.

Hoederer, by contrast, is the revolutionist who has discarded all illusions. He has gained complete mastery over himself, no longer affected by personal considerations. Sartre admires this type of Communist: his capacity for making decisions and resolutely acting upon them, his inflexibility of purpose, his devotion to the truth, his freedom from all forms of self-deception. To Hugo, however, the typical Existentialist hero, nothing seems real, not even his wife. He is a wretched performer on the closed-in stage of his own mind, full of tormenting inner conflicts. Though Hoederer has already begun negotiations that are supposed to be treasonable, Hugo is still unable to act. He is puzzled by the abstract logic of the situation: the crucial decision which will transmit the signal to his hand to pull the trigger. Hoederer, on the other hand, is not at all troubled by abstract principles. The Communist Party, he maintains, is organized to seize power, regardless of the means employed. That is the underlying aim and purpose, even if for the time being a policy of "compromise" must be expediently adopted. When Hugo accuses him of class collaboration, he retorts that the Party is only a tool; it is not strong enough at present to effect the revolutionary seizure of power. If it is necessary to lie and swindle in order to achieve his goal, he will lie and swindle. There is nothing strange in such an attitude. The Party has always told expedient lies, and who, for that matter, can say that he has never told lies to himself. Hoederer, in short, suffers from no scruples of conscience. The art of lying grows out of the evil tensions of life in a class-structured society. Once the class system of economic exploitation is abolished, the necessity to lie will vanish. Insofar as he is concerned, the revolutionary fight is waged not against men or principles but solely against the oppressors. Cheerfully he admits that he has "dirty hands," plunged right up to the elbow in filth and blood. It is impossible to govern innocently—a theme that is developed with greater resourcefulness and complexity of tragic insight in *The Devil and the Good Lord*.

It is this irreconcilable conflict between Party ruthlessness and the call of conscience that deepens the tragic impact of *Dirty Hands*. Hugo joined the Party because he felt it represented the cause of justice. When it ceases to be that, he is resolved to leave it. He is not interested in accepting men as they are, only for what they can become. Hoederer loves them for what they are in their common struggle against suffering and death. He castigates Hugo as the type of intellectual who despises mankind because at heart he despises himself. That is why the intellectual never makes a good revolutionary. Convinced of Hugo's infirmity of will, he deliberately turns his back on him, but Hugo is saddled with too active an imagination to be a killer. He is aware of his inner uncertainty. He could never have killed Hoederer for purely "objective" reasons. Only when he finds Hoederer making love to his wife does he shoot him. The power of jealousy is stronger than the dictates of political duty.

Now Hugo perceives that it was pure chance which killed Hoederer. The undercutting irony of the play is strengthened when he discovers that the "counter-revolutionary" policy for which Hoederer was condemned to death, is now the official Party line. His "sacrifice" had been all for naught, but he refuses to disclaim responsibility for his deed by assuming another name. He pays the price by his willingness to die at the end. In that way he will know that Hoederer did not perish in vain. It is this insight which gives him the courage to meet the assassins. He is beyond redemption as a Communist. He remains self-deceived.

Literary Existentialism thus highlights the tragic ambiguities and ironies of the human situation. The contradictions at the heart of life are not to be glossed over by a system of economic determinism. The Existentialist writer does not hide from "the truth of life and death." He knows "the indifference and the sovereign importance of each man and all men." [4] Man chooses his own ends, even though he realizes there are no absolute standards. In the farce, *Nekrassov*, that wittily satirizes the hysterical fear the French rulers have of Communism, Georges de Valéra, the confidence man, declares like a good Existentialist: "Good and evil, I take it all upon myself. I am responsible for everything." [5]

The Blood of Others, by Simone de Beauvoir, a disciple of Sartre, offers a good example of how an Existentialist novel handles a revolutionary theme. Upon each character is thrust an inescapable burden of responsibility. Jean, the son of a highly respected bourgeois family, leaves home in order to devote himself to the Communist cause, but he is soon disillusioned. Henceforth he will not obey Party orders. Hélène, the woman who dies fighting in the Resistance movement, is opposed to the Communist doctrine that behavior is conditioned solely by external circumstances. What a person is depends on himself alone. She resents being pigeonholed within a class; she prefers to believe in her own uniqueness. Throughout the story she is haunted by the mystery of self-identity, the secret of the grammatical fiction "I" that will one day disintegrate into nothingness. Jean, true to his convictions, refuses to become embroiled in dirty politics; he will not treat mankind as if it were a mass of dough to be kneaded into shape. But when the crisis comes, their scruples are overcome. When the Germans occupy France, both Hélène and Jean decide to collaborate with the Communists in fighting the common enemy. Theirs is a choice freely made. Jean plans acts of reprisal and terrorism even though innocent people will be made to suffer. At last he is fulfilling a personal destiny he has himself decided upon.

In the Existentialist conception of the tragic, the hero, whether revolutionary or intellectual, strives for freedom; he is responsible for both his failures and his achievements. Sartre attacks Communism on the ground that it disposes of good and evil as pseudo problems. The occupation of France, the fact of torture, the existence of concentration camps, the use of crematoria, brought home to writers the reality of evil. No longer could they view the situation from a safe aesthetic distance and, uncommitted, indulge in the luxury of psychological and moral relativism. Even in this period of national humiliation and horror, when revolt meant death, men were willing to risk their lives in the name of an ideal which would bring them in closer solidarity to their kind. Literature had of necessity to deal with the moral problem, and morality was politics. In this world crisis—and Existentialism is a literature of crisis—the novel and the drama had to be used as symbolic forms of action.

Though Sartre espoused revolutionary politics, he did not wish the writer to be converted into an ideological tool of the Communist Party. Art must have its roots in human freedom. Literature must remain fundamentally moral and hence autonomous. Man is free; his insecurity springs from the need imposed on him to choose himself at every moment. He is basically what he does; no one can point out for him the road he must travel. The contemporary situation in which he finds himself conditions but does not *determine* his choice. The tragic hero makes his past and present in the light of his future projects. In showing that the moral imperative is in each case contingent upon a human decision, Sartre invests his plays with a pervasive atmosphere of tragic irony.[6]

Sartre cannot seem to make up his mind exactly where he stands in relation to the Communist movement. He admits the truth of the Marxist diagnosis that Existentialism is an historical, class-conditioned manifestation.

> Existentialism, in its contemporary form, appears with the decomposition of the bourgeoisie, and its origin is bourgeois. But that this decomposition can *disclose* certain aspects of the human condition and make possible certain metaphysical intuitions does not mean that these intuitions and this disclosure are illusions of the bourgeois consciousness or mythical representations of the situation.[7]

Sartre, who makes too much of a concession at this point, is trying hard to fit the doctrinaire Marxist conceptual system within an Existentialist framework. Actually he cannot get himself to believe in the divinely appointed "mission" of the proletariat, its imputed state of efficacious grace, yet he continues to insist that the fate of literature is tied up today with the fate of the workers.

His creative work is better than his theoretical pronouncements. He will not transform Existentialist literature into an instrument of propaganda. Uncompromisingly dedicated to the tragic truth of life, the writer must be outspoken in his opposition to all forms of injustice.

Man is a becoming and therefore never to be identified with what he is at any given moment. Bad faith consists in the pretence that morals have been fixed from the beginning of time, that they are universal and prescriptive, whereas they really represent a human choice. It is by his actions that the tragic hero, responsible for himself, changes the incomprehensible and absurd world of things into a world charged with human meanings. Hence Existentialist man confronts the tragic contingency of existence without the spirit of righteousness.

The vision of the absurd is never absent in Sartre's work, and it fills the tragic hero with dread. The tragic conflict emerges in the fight against the myth of absurdity. In his plays Sartre emphasizes the contrast between a Nature that is without purpose and the moral imperative that governs human affairs. This conflict, which Sartre views from the perspective of irony, raises the question whether the intellectual who looks upon the world as meaningless is justified in urging upon mankind an ideal that it cannot hope to achieve objectively. According to Sartre, the intellectual is on the side of the Revolution because only thus can he save himself and be restored to social reality. He must ally himself with the working class, even though he cannot accept the Marxist interpretation of history and its behavioristic conception of man.

Sartre has never explicitly worked out the implications of Marxism in its bearings on the problem of tragedy. The internal dialectical tensions of his plays and novels, however, make clear his awareness that the ideological precepts of Marxism, if rigorously followed, would undermine the basis of the tragic vision. It is on the fundamental issue of the freedom of the will that Sartre breaks with the Marxist synthesis. The hero he presents in his dramas and fiction is caught in a situation that is not only ambiguous but paradoxical. He is not a "positive hero." He is the man marching toward death, the source of values, the foundation of his own being.

He beholds the opacity of existence; he strips off the veils of appearance and sees things in their obscene na-

kedness; he experiences "nausea." The metaphysical ver-
tigo that overcomes him springs from his perception of
the unconquerable absurdity of existence. Roquentin
loathes existence but his flesh binds him to this earth and
he cannot escape. The heart of reality opens up before
him but the revelation is only a negative epiphany.
Things are what they are, incomprehensible. Nothing can
change the gratuitousness of existence, neither revolutionary action nor the writing of a book. Even as Roquentin
writes his diary, he is, like André Gorz in *The Traitor*,
suspicious of literature. Thoughts betray, each truth is
subjectively conditioned, particular and relative. Consciousness, in its attempt to lift itself above the contingent and rise to the plane of the universal, is abstract,
disincarnate, a futile question mark hurled at the sphinx
of being. Consciousness consents to its own defeat. It is,
as André Gorz puts it, "consciousness of nothingness . . .
which spontaneously tends . . . to produce itself as an
object; it cries, dreams, and, by choice, writes; it creates
literary objects in which it substitutes its own nothingness." [8]

This creative activity only intensifies the malaise of
subjectivity. It rests on the assumption that thought can
conquer the world, that literature can transform nothingness into a triumph of transcendence. Literature is thus
a strategy of evasion. The writer plays a part in this duplicity, searching for a total consciousness that will elevate
him above the finite. The tragic vision he shadows forth
reflects his own existential contradictions. The Existentialist hero wants to be a man joined in action with other
men but finds himself locked up in a self-built dungeon
of ideas and introspections. He has no individuality; he
suffers from a profound horror of "I." He is a negativity
that speaks and acts, though knowing that his efforts will
not materially affect the future course of history.

There is no contradiction between Sartre's belief that
life is contingent and gratuitous and his commitment to
the revolutionary cause. Since no form of existence is necessary, each man must choose his own life. The only thing

that binds men together is their metaphysical condition, the finitude of existence. Though Sartre is ambiguous in his attitude toward the Communist Party, he defines his position as being that of a Marxist, but he is no docile fellow traveler. In the final analysis, Marxism formulates a myth of revolutionary violence that must be believed, since the belief is capable of generating the will to action. Sartre's view of life, however, remains tragic. He is opposed to a Marxism that ignores the existential decision which can sustain man in his struggle to change the world in the name of justice. Sartre points out that the Communist who blindly obeys the dictates of the Party is renouncing his personal birthright of freedom. It is the human condition, not the class struggle, which for Sartre constitutes the absolute in history.[9] And it is the human condition which, as we shall try to show in our analysis of Malraux's fiction, is the generative source of the tragic vision.

IT IS principally the novel that imaginatively comes to
grips with the stormy passions of politics that convulse
the modern world. Novels like *Man's Fate, Darkness at
Noon, The Seed Beneath the Snow, For Whom the Bell
Tolls, Bread and Wine* reflect the incredible conflicts
generated by an age that is hypnotically under the spell
of a political myth: the myth of revolutionary violence.
Ideology enters as a constitutive element into the substance and structure of fiction. Those novelists who hewed
to the Party line and exploited literature as a political
weapon produced work that was necessarily partisan in
tone. To the extent that it was propagandistic it lacked the
tragic complexity of insight and motivation that Dostoevski revealed in *The Possessed*. Only when the writer resolutely faces, as Arthur Koestler does in *Darkness at Noon*,
the contradictions implicit in the myth of revolution, the
peculiar temptations that beset him, can he convey some
intimation of the tragic struggle that is fought out in the
soul of the revolutionary hero. He must attempt to disclose, without distortion or evasion, the formidable obstacles, human as well as social, that stand in the way of
the revolutionary consummation: the evils that invariably
attend the effort to realize ideal ends, the corruption of
conscience wrought by the "principled" violation of ethical norms, the sense of the tragic element in history that
Vico discerned.[1]

Malraux introduces Existentialist heroes who, like
Stavrogin, suffer intensely from the malady of alienation,

though unlike him they are able to commit themselves. They cannot believe in the promise of immortality, in the Savior who came down to earth for the redemption of sinful mankind. For them God is dead. Alone with themselves, shut up within the cell of their own ego, they face a universe that is without a glimmer of ultimate meaning. The central characters in *The Conquerors* go ahead with their ritual of sacrifice even as they become aware of the certainty of failure and the absurdity of their actions. In presenting characters tormented by the insoluble problem of consciousness, Malraux reminds one of Dostoevski. In his work there is present the same brooding sense of metaphysical terror, the same feverish speculation about matters of ultimate concern, the same desire to penetrate regions of awareness inaccessible to the "normal" self. Malraux pictures the darkness of the earthly prison in which his heroes, in despair, act out their absurd destiny. It is despair that drives them to revolt and it is despair that defeats them. But though they are dragged under in the end, their revolt grants them a moment of vision that presents a victory, however brief, of the human spirit.

This is the nature of the conflict that sustains Malraux's tragic vision. The fiction Malraux published during the twenties and thirties anticipates many of the themes later developed in Existentialist novels. Though Malraux's heroes are inevitably doomed, they will not surrender the sovereignty of self. And yet they struggle, like Claude and Perken in *The Royal Way*, to subdue the perverse pride of self. The rebel as "conqueror" gets caught deeper in the contradictions of his own being; he cannot impose his will upon alien reality and he cannot escape from the realm of nature. He faces a great void: the knowledge that everything is absurd. He bears his fate with unfaltering courage, even though the emptiness in his heart reflects the emptiness of the universe. Opposed to a world that excludes the human and allows room only for the dark and destructive triumph of death, man nevertheless asserts the integrity of his will.

The self of the heroes, in *The Royal Way* as in *The Conquerors*, is at war with itself; selfhood is a weary burden to be cast off, and yet the self searches for a way of life that will neutralize the absurdity of existence. The quest is always in vain. The self encounters an external world that is ageless, a graveyard of ruins. Death is the final conqueror. In *The Royal Way*, which takes place in the jungles of Cambodia and Siam, the sense of selfhood is extinguished. Decay is universal. Death is the supreme mystery which only the power of art, and that only for a luminous moment, can overcome. The novel exposes the cruel deceptions life practices upon its human victims. Claude and Perken are both preoccupied with the finality of death which nullifies all ambition. They will, however, continue to fight for their beliefs, even though weighed down by a fundamental skepticism as to the value of all human endeavor. In their bitter realization of the uselessness of striving and in their paradoxical affirmation of the unconquerable human will, they betray their devotion to the mystique of action, the only antidote they can find for the tragic insight that life for the individual is utterly shorn of meaning. The background of the Asiatic jungle, with its spawn of insects and teeming animal life, its subhuman savages, its enervating heat, reinforces the greatness of the human soul that has the courage to carry out its dream in the face of death. In this lies the indisputable greatness of man: his dedication to the life of action, his steadfast loyalty even when threatened with disaster.

Only through the sacramental bond of loyalty, as illustrated by the strange friendship of Claude and Perken, is the eternal loneliness of the human soul lifted. Perken is not afraid of dying. What he finds intolerable is that death lies outside the will of man; it bears witness to the fatality of the human condition. Perken realizes his helplessness and yet he must protest against the indifference of the universe; he strives to assert the meaning of his existence but his struggle is futile. He cannot defeat death, which is not a culmination but a lifelong process. With sensitive insight and compassion Malraux delineates the essential dignity of man, however wretched his condition. And this craving for the assertion of one's dignity as a man manifests itself in a multitude of ways: in love and hate, sacrifice and revenge, life and death.

Malraux's novels represent a distinguished achievement in that they are revolutionary in theme without ever becoming doctrinaire in content. *The Conquerors*, though it deals with the revolutionary organization of the Chinese masses in Canton, is primarily interested in depicting the character of two professional revolutionists: Garine and Borodin. Malraux, like Koestler in *Darkness at Noon*, shows that there are obligations more binding than unconditional party obedience. The revolutionary leader must be disciplined but he must also preserve his integrity as an individual. Orders are often issued by men who are concerned solely with the seizure of power, without regard for such moral considerations as justice or pity. Indeed, Malraux shows that the professional revolutionist, by the very nature of his activity, must be prepared to commit any action that is "good" for the cause, without being deterred by scruples of conscience. In brief, he must, like Hoederer, be ready to go beyond questions of good and evil, since in the end power justifies itself. The conqueror, by dictating his own terms, shapes the course of history.

The individual leader is nevertheless compelled to face his own internal contradictions. No two men conform to a single dialectical formula. There is the rub: each individual is a special case. The reactionary clings stubbornly to the force of tradition, the saint preaches the gospel of nonresistance, the traitor will, for a price, betray the people. The terrorists, impatient of all restraints and the pressures of *Realpolitik*, demand the blood of the oppressors. The masses, filled with destructive hatred, long to reassume the dignity that is theirs as a natural right but in their deluded ignorance become the prey of some demagogue. Malraux creates a fictional universe that reveals life in all its refractory mysteriousness, human nature that is ambivalent, capable of the noblest act of sacrifice and the vilest treachery.

All this, in *The Conquerors*, is presented without any attempt to glorify the character of the masses or their leaders. Garine, for example, entertains no illusions about his "love" for the people. He knows full well what base instincts are part of the nature of man and must be accepted as such. If he chooses to fight for the liberation of the masses it is not because he clings to any mystical conception of historic necessity but merely because they are the conquered: the insulted and injured. "Yes, and because, on the whole, they have more heart, they are more humane than the others; they possess the virtues of the vanquished." [2] This attitude of sympathy for the oppressed stems, of course, from Dostoevski; it is a humanitarian rather than specifically Marxist motif. [3] Garine also knows that once the people acquire power they, too, will become grasping, corrupt, cruel, and contemptible. He is under no sentimental illusions. As a revolutionary he cannot throw off the painful contradiction of his life: while he hated all forms of service, he was now in thrall to a discipline that demanded everything of him, even the impossible. Why should he assume this thankless burden of duty? Perhaps he was driven by a secret lust for power. The absolutism of the revolutionary organization repels him. Men are not machines to be ideologically wound up and manipulated. At the end he arrives at the tragic insight that one cannot possess life without the metaphysical realization that everything on earth is futile. It is his confrontation of the myth of the absurd that enables him to overcome the weakness of pity and identifies him as a tragic figure.

In *Man's Fate*, too, the tragic hero proceeds with his revolutionary activity, though he knows he is doomed. For him revolt is a fate voluntarily embraced, a willed martyrdom. Despite his knowledge that existence is absurd, he dies for the sake of life, not because of any love for death. That is how he invests life with a meaning that transcends the biological instinct of survival. Though *Man's Fate* describes the abortive uprising of the workers and the bloody suppression of the revolutionary movement by Chiang Kai-shek, it is not, strictly speaking, a political novel. It offers a devastating criticism of the policy followed by the Communist Party, its use of expediency in pursuing its long-range plan for the seizure of power. Malraux is imaginatively setting forth not an ideological thesis but a tragic humanism. These revolutionary fighters are actuated by a variety of motives, but basically what they are willing to die for is the condition of man: he must cease to be degraded. He must be accorded dignity, but that will be accomplished only when he is no longer an object of economic exploitation. It is in the name of this ideal that Kyo, one of the protagonists in *Man's Fate*, is ready to give up his life.

The characters in *Man's Fate* are swayed by impulses of which they are unconscious; they wonder at times about the motives that lead them to act. They keep faith with the myth that bids them sacrifice their life. Malraux makes it clear that there are many myths to which men can, and do, devote themselves: alcohol, pleasure, sex, conquest, destruction, creativity, religion. Each myth exercises its specific spell and appeals to temperaments of a given type. Indeed, as Gisors, the father of Kyo, points out, the age suffers from mythomania. In the light of the eternity that swallows up all the passions and illusions of men, who is to say which myth holds out the greatest blessing. One myth is as foolish as another; opium is as good as action. His son, rising above the temptation of contemplative thought, plunges into action in behalf of a meaning that he chooses to affirm. The revolutionaries, having made their peace with death, are not afraid to die. Katov and Kyo carry in reserve a pellet of cyanide which they will use if captured rather than endure horrible torture at the sands of the enemy. When the uprising has been put down and the workers and their leaders are taken captive, Katov, in a magnificent gesture of sacrifice, turns over his precious drug—the quick death—to two Chinese fellow revolutionaries.

Man's Fate is the carrier of the tragic vision in that it affirms an ethic of human responsibility, the will to human dignity, in the face of the incurable absurdity of existence. The revolutionary novel *par excellence,* it is instinct with implications that make it anti-Marxist in content. No single truth about life is valid; all value-judgments are relative, many mythic perspectives may be chosen, but not one of them can escape the knowledge that death is final. *Man's Fate* reveals how men of different temperaments confront the fatality of death. It is this motif that is always present: the consciousness that men are mortal. Sustained by his faith in the brotherhood of man and by his hope that it will ultimately triumph, the revolutionary transcends the limitations of his finite ego. No matter what he is made to suffer, his sacrifice stands justified. It is the power of this hope that makes it possible for him to die with grace.

This pervasive theme of death lends tragic tension to the development of the plot. These revolutionaries are, like the terrorists, brought face to face with the absolute of death. *Man's Fate* begins, appropriately enough, with Ch'en in the darkness and solitude of night preparing like a sacrificial priest to slay the chosen victim. He must act, he must kill this sleeping man, even while he is overcome with anguish and guilt and the knowledge that death ends all. What he experiences in the emptiness of night is not fear but dread: "he was alone with death, alone in a place without men, limply crushed by horror and by the taste of blood." [4]

Unlike Ch'en, Kyo, one of the organizers of the insurrection, would not kill except in battle. The living embodiment of the revolutionary saint, he is disciplined, his self sternly subordinated to the needs of the cause, the struggle of the workers to establish a Soviet China. He is will incarnate, but the rebel within him, even as he keeps it under control, is not inactive. He rebels against the absolutism and infallibility of the Party, the restraints it imposes, its doctrine of historic necessity. He knows that Marxism offers no cure. The subjective self remains unredeemed in the revolutionary struggle for power. Nevertheless, he gives himself wholly to the call and compulsion of his mythomania: to release in this way the innate dignity of his people, for there lay the destiny of the world. Kyo is not one to spout Marxist principles. On the contrary, he knows the meaning of solitude even when engaged in revolutionary work: "the inescapable aloneness behind the living multitude like the great primitive night behind dense, low night under which this city of deserted streets was expectantly waiting, full of hope and hatred." [5] Not even love can cure this anguish of aloneness.

Ch'en, too, when he comes to Gisors for spiritual solace, confesses his terrible sense of aloneness after the murder he had committed. While plunging the knife into the body of the victim he had felt not only horror but something else, something closely related to the question he raises: "What about death?" Death—that posits an insoluble problem. Gisors begins to suspect the truth, namely, that Ch'en is inwardly fascinated by a life of terrorism, that perhaps he is driven by an overwhelming desire to be killed. Ch'en seeks no glory, no happiness, and therefore death is his highest court of appeal, to be invested with the meaning that others give to life. Death is his fatality. Obsessed by his idea, he would dive deeper and deeper into the red-rimmed world of murder and never return from it alive. In the end he would inevitably be caught, tortured, and put to death. As Gisors perceives, this young man could not accept an ideology which he could not transform immediately into action. Ideas merely thought, not lived, were ineffectual. Had Gisors himself not taught the young students, most of them members of the petty bourgeoisie, that Marxism is an expression of the will of the proletarians to know themselves and to conquer? Now in his old age he realizes how little we can comprehend the secret soul of others, how inescapably alone each man is.

Convinced it is immortal, the Party pursues its unalterable purpose, willing to suffer temporary setbacks. Ch'en, who is governed by his passion for destruction, feels no bond with the workers who are being armed for the struggle. He knew he would die alone. Even in the heat of battle, while his comrades lie slain in the middle of the street, he feels no bond of communion between himself and his men. He is not one of them. He cannot get rid of his solitude.

Nor can he unhesitatingly obey the orders of the Party. The only way in which he can come to terms with himself is to kill. Kyo cannot understand Ch'en's fascination with death, the ecstasy he derives from deeds of terrorism, an ecstasy heightened by the anticipation of his own death. This was madness. In desiring to kill Chiang Kai-shek, Ch'en is not looking for peace; he wants to reduce the sum total of human suffering. When the first attempt at assassination fails to come off, he resolves to kill himself in the act and thus make sure that his plan will succeed; he will hurl himself with the bomb under the car. The decision ends his private anguish. The decision to die is, like Kaliayev's resolution of his conflict in *The Just Assassins*, an expression of his freedom. He will pay for the murder with his own life. Gisors voices the theme of the novel when he says: "all that men are willing to die for, beyond self-interest, tends more or less obscurely to justify that fate by giving it a foundation in dignity." [6] That is Kyo's belief, too. The most powerful motivating force in man is his desire to be more than man, to rise above his human condition, to fulfill his dream of becoming God.

Whereas Ch'en is consumed by the neurotic need to organize terrorism as a mystic cult, Kyo is the master of his death, as Malraux puts it, and therefore free. He will live only on conditions he is willing to accept. His sacrificial courage grows out of his faith that "communism will make dignity possible for those whom I am fighting." [7] He had seen men die and "he had always thought that it is fine to die by one's hand, a death that resembled one's life. And to die is passivity, but to kill oneself is action." [8] He kills himself, he swallows the cyanide, with full consciousness of the meaning of what he is doing; his death is a martyrdom, a conquest of death that is transfigured with the light of love. Because he accepts the burden of his fate as a man, he consents to his own death. "He had fought for what in his time was charged with the deepest meaning and the greatest hope; he was dying among those with whom he would have wanted to live; he was dying, like each of these men, because he had given a meaning to his life. What would have been the value of a life for which he would not have been willing to die? [9] Here is the tragic epiphany of revolutionary sacrifice: the attempt to justify the ordeal of suffering and the destiny of death. His will at this last moment is in perfect control. For him dying could be "an exalted act, the supreme expression of a life which this death so much resembled." [10] Though the insurrection fails and Kyo dies, the novel ends on a note of affirmation.

This type of tragic afirmation is not one calculated to satisfy Communist critics. They assail Malraux on the ground that he is an Existentialist, lost in a cloud of metaphysical despair. It is his awareness of the aloneness of man and his obsession with the fact of death—it is this that makes him the literary spokesman of a dying culture. His characters are culpably confined in the void of solitude and even when they are involved in the class struggle they contemplate only their own forlorn image of self. Even anguish is hopelessly personal and subjective, instead of being rooted in the soil of capitalist oppression. In short, the indictment reads, Malraux, instead of concentrating on man in relation to his socio-economic environment, focuses attention primarily on the metaphysically alienated man. He pictures a world that is morally aimless and meaningless—and that is sheer treason. Action is taken solely for the sake of action. "Freedom, which in Sartre confronts nothingness, is the corridor to death in Malraux." [11] In fact, "everything in Malraux's work flows into death." [12] Death is made the underlying measure of life. What Roger Garaudy's polemic, Literature of the Graveyard, denounces as a species of "reactionary" defeatism is the vindication of Malraux's genius as a tragic novelist.

Malraux's fiction adds a tragic dimension to the myth of the absurd. The hero faces a world that is incomprehensible, incommensurate with his live consciousness, and yet he must invest it with the order of meaning. Malraux senses the mystery that is beyond the power of art, revolutionary or Existentialist, to capture; it can only suggest that which lies beyond phenomenal reality. The dialogue that he establishes "between the demoniac in contemporary man and his world and a transcendent reality which has taken on the negative value of an absence and become a source of anguish and obsession, is a powerful realization in negative form of an act of faith. It is a tragic realization born out of a sense of the absolute which allows of no direct positive expression." [13] Malraux's tragic realization affirms the autonomy of art, the created work as the sovereign source of meaning. But the void the writer encounters and wrestles with is never conquered; struggle as he may, he cannot, like his imaginary creations, rise above the phenomenal world that screens the absolute. This is the spiritual dilemma out of which Malraux forges his form of the tragic vision, one that comes closest to the idea of it we have sought to elicit in this study.

13 CONCLUSION

TWENTIETH-CENTURY fiction and drama are faced with a task of staggering complexity: how to give shape and substance to the myth of nothingness. The modern literary consciousness must attempt to distil the transcendent passion of the tragic out of a radical negativity, the nature of which we have analyzed in the preceding chapters. The tragic vision, since it grows out of nihilistic premises, is confronted at the outset with a paradox: the writer presents a hero who, though recognizing the uselessness of all human effort, nevertheless strives to affirm his human freedom and his solidarity with doomed mankind. He refuses to lie about the truth of the human condition, and his refusal represents a gesture of defiance. Hemingway's heroes, for example, know that *nada* (or nothing) is a Something, a reality, but they will not submit to the tyranny of the absurd.[1] The tragic writer of our time works his way out of this dilemma by viewing the human condition in the perspective of irony, without surrendering either his nihilism or his existential commitments.

The creative mind is kindled into activity by its perception of the conflict between two planes of being, the finite and the infinite, what Arthur Koestler calls the trivial and the tragic. The first is the realm of the familiar, the mundane, the diurnal, which includes the recurrent cycles of routine and the minutiae of behavior; the second seeks to discern the indwelling order of the universe, the ultimate cause of being, the dimension of eternity, the meaning of fate. One is relative, the other absolute. The first, broadly speaking, lends itself to comedy, the second to tragedy. The two planes intersect. Though the artist endeavors to fuse them in the crucible of the imagination they stubbornly resist his efforts to unify them.

Most men spend practically all their life on the plane of the trivial, fleeing from the threat of disaster and the knowledge of death, but they cannot always avoid the sudden intrusion of the tragic into the even, reassuring rhythm of their days. If they confront the challenge courageously, we then witness the birth of the tragic sense. However, in an age that is overshadowed by the myth of Sisyphus, the tragic vision cannot be captured in its essential purity of form. It is inevitably mixed with ironic overtones. The artist "experiences the trivial in the perspective of the tragic, in the light of 'eternity looking through time,' and therein can probably be found the essence of the artist's approach." [2] Therein, too, can be found the fruitful uses of tragic irony.

Kierkegaard, as we pointed out, taught a number of writers the value of the art of irony in all its existential complexity, especially as it enters into the stream of indirect communication. Kierkegaard was tensely aware of the painful contradictions that beset the mind as it soars to the infinite while existence binds it fast to the finite, and he searched desperately for a way of reconciling the two realms. In indirect communication the writer is forced to rely on the subtle and difficult device of irony, which springs from the dismaying insight that "the phenomenon is not reality but the opposite of reality." For the purpose of concealment or provocation, statements compounded of dialectical irony are enormously useful. According to Kierkegaard, irony is "a mode of existence, and there is nothing more absurd than to suppose that it is a manner of speech, or for an author to congratulate himself on having here and there expressed himself ironically. Whoever essentially possesses irony possesses it as long as the day lasts, and it is fettered to no form because it is the expression in him, of infinity." [3]

More important in its bearing on our central theme is Kierkegaard's description of the way the ironic mode is related to the three stages of the aesthetic, the ethical, and the religious. Only between the first two stages does there subsist the meditating power of irony; between the last two there emerges the play of humor. "Irony arises," Kierkegaard declares, "from the constant placing of the particularities of the finite together with the infinite ethical requirement, thus permitting the contradiction to come into being." [4] The ethicist, who closely resembles the heroes who appear in the fiction of Malraux and in the plays of Sartre, falls back upon irony as his indispensable means of grasping "the contradiction between the manner in which he exists inwardly, and the fact that he does not outwardly express it." [5]

Through the sustaining method of irony, the romantic writer punishes his boundless expectations, the folly of his Promethean revolt. Through irony he cures himself in part of the virulent disease of romanticism. The infinite beckons the modern tragic hero while reason mocks his nostalgia for the absolute. For him the absolute has become the symbolic equivalent of the Nothingness that Heidegger explores in *Sein und Zeit*. The vision of that which lies beyond the limits of *nada* may lead him completely away from the borders of reality. Since he is defeated time and again in his metaphysical quest, he safeguards himself against bitter disillusionment by viewing himself and his situation in an ironic light. Kierkegaard learned to laugh at his own aches and pains, his compulsive and often morbid habit of introspection. The double vision he possessed, the power of looking upon everything in life microscopically as well as macroscopically, was richly productive of irony. Hence he could confess that the paradox "is really the *pathos* of intellectual life." [6]

We have tried to show that in our time of trouble the tragic vision cannot function without some admixture of irony. By means of ironic counterpointing the tragic experience is neither annulled nor transcended but some-how qualitatively transformed. Pain is not pain, failure is not entirely failure. It is not that the categories of mean-ing and the operative table of values are so confounded that no standards of judgment remain, but they cannot today be affirmed with the old certitude. The categories are seen to be ambiguous, equivocal, and paradoxical. Ev-erything is bathed in the chiaroscuro of relativism and uncertainty. Standing at the edge of doom, man struggles to discover a meaning though he is doubtful that one can be found. Perhaps he is tragic only in his own eyes. Per-haps the only meaning to be elicited is the one his con-sciousness invents. The tragic humanism that a Malraux or Camus embraces has purged itself of all theistic hopes.

On a higher plane, irony becomes an inescapable con-stituent of the tragic vision when the hero rashly sets out to dethrone the gods. Ruled by his intellect, he seeks to pluck out the mystery of nature. Dwelling henceforth in the confines of history, he insists that the truth must be told. Following Nietzsche's lead, he comes to the fright-ening realization that he must depend on no one but himself. He resorts to the weapon of irony to enable him to endure his fate. He can laugh at his own sorry predica-ment. Let the vulture gnaw at his liver, let the monstrous serpent coil around him—he will not abandon his ironic sense of life, his gift of freedom that makes for defiance.

Fundamentally irony springs from the knowledge that comedy and tragedy emanate from the same existential source. Once the vision of the world is relativized, then everything depends on the point of view from which the writer observes and interprets the welter of experience in the time-space continuum. He specializes in what has loosely been called the irony of fate. Events fail to live up to human expectations. The ideal the tragic hero pursues with such single-mindedness of purpose is balked by the fell clutch of circumstance, the effect of contingency. He must face the appalling contrast between illusion and reality. He realizes that reason is the slave, not the mas-ter, of life. Thus he learns to laugh at his own absurd myths and vital fictions, even going so far as to apotheosize the absurd. He must place his faith in the constructions of his own mind that he well knows do not correspond with the order of reality.

Ours is preeminently an age of tragic irony. The irony is implicit in the dominant mode of metaphysical interrogation and defiance that pervades the work of such writers as Kafka, Malraux, Camus, Gide, Eugene O'Neill, and Samuel Beckett. In an age of science, an age in which psychoanalysis exposes the demonic contradictions of the unconscious, the writer is obsessed by the irrationalities of existence. Polarity is the law of life, paradox is the soul of indirect communication, irony is the heartbeat of meaning. Feeling is held in check by thought, intuition by reason, the spirit by the degrading necessities of the flesh, life by death, the absolute by the reality of nothingness. The difficulty of reconciling the tragic vision with an ironic perspective is caused by the modern writer's nihilistic commitment. He falls back, as we have said, on irony as a necessary device for making the pain of life bearable. He knows that nothing will be changed by his questions, his revolt against the absurd, his existential commitment to life, but he goes ahead just the same. Irony is an expression of metaphysical rebellion that is aware of its own futility. Because life is absurd and death an intolerable outrage, the modern writer raises his voice in frenzied denunciation that is balanced and kept under control by the art of irony, though the irony in itself remains a type of defiance.

Eugene O'Neill was convinced that it was impossible for modern man to find a faith that would satisfy the claims of reason. O'Neill faced the truth of life as he saw it and sought to affirm the potential greatness of man who struggles to achieve fulfillment on his own terms. O'Neill knew that no single outlook pointed the way to a final truth. Like Ibsen, however, he never gave up the quest for meaning and truth, insisting that men must face the truth about themselves. Man presumes to question not only himself but all of being. He realizes he enjoys no privileged status on earth, but the act of questioning raises issues which he cannot avoid. His metaphysical query constitutes a Heideggerian "leap," which enables him to thrust away "all the previous security, whether real or fancied, of life." [7] By asking the question, he penetrates to the root of being; he is asking the question behind all the questions man can ask: "Why the why?" [8]

O'Neill projects one aspect of this universal conflict in his Expressionistic play, *The Great God Brown*, in which Dion Anthony symbolizes the destiny of the artist in America, alone, misunderstood, split within his own being, driven by spiritual yearnings which he cannot fulfill or even reveal. Unable to adjust to a world that is based exclusively on materialistic values, he deliberately destroys himself. Only by resorting to savage irony can he protect himself against people. Life is torment and ecstasy, suffering and ineffable joy. As he grows older, his face loses its Pan-like quality and turns Mephistophelean. There is no God to whom he can turn for comfort. When he evinces signs of jealousy of the Great God Brown, who has started to keep Cybel, the prostitute who is the symbol of Mother Earth, she tells him: "What makes you pretend you think love is so important, anyway? It's just one of a lot of things you do to keep life living." [9] Life is not important. Only what is inside a man, his spirit, is important; the rest belongs to the earth. When Dion is terrified by the thought of the end ("To feel one's life blown out like the flame of a cheap match." [10]), it is Cybel who cries out: "What's the use of bearing children? What's the use of giving birth to death?" [11] The tragic hero, in O'Neill's plays as in the literature of Existentialism, faces the unmeaning of a universe that is not supported by absolute values.

ii

The primary aim of this book is not to discuss philosophy, Existentialism, the nature of time and death, the new conception of the self that has arisen, the political myths that today compete for the minds of men, but to picture in all its dialectical complexity of opposition the struggle to communicate the tragic vision in twentieth-century literature. We have examined the background of forces that inhibit its expression, the quality of modern consciousness that militates against the emergence of a full-throated affirmation of life. We have tried to do more than analyze the impact and interaction of ideologies in our time. The second section of the book attempts to show how these underlie and enter as constitutive elements into the warp and woof of those literary works that are informed with a tragic content. The tragic vision is shadowed forth in those novels or plays that portray man's persistent, if in the end unavailing, struggle to impose meaning on his life. The tragic hero knows or suspects that there is no justification for his commitment, his act of sacrifice, no reason why he should endanger or yield his life for a given cause in a universe that is indifferent to his needs, his quest for meaning. He rejects all superhuman standards. Spurning the aid of the absolute, he depends entirely on his own powers and on his free decisions as to how these powers are to be employed. Life is henceforth its own meaning. Here are the prescribed limits within which the modern tragic conflict must be worked out. There is no universal order that the tragic hero can recognize and embrace as his own, only an order that is alien, contingent, and incomprehensible. The laws of Nature are not the laws of man. The world is meaningless, and yet he must somehow affirm life and, if possible, justify it.

But if all art, whatever its subjective intention, celebrates the indestructible continuity of existence and represents a spiritual victory, however temporary, over the forces of darkness, the writer must determine the dialectical relation that obtains between his nihilistic *Weltanschauung* and the tragic vision. That is the heart of the matter. Once he encounters the vision of the absurd, he must root himself in uncertainty. The questions he propounds in his work are more revealing than the answers he gives, but the questions point to his irrepressible need to rebel against the fate of the absurd. He would fain preserve those finite values in which he believes, even if in the end they do not prevail. Goodness does not triumph, justice is not the ruling principle in life. The modern tragic hero, however, does come to realize the nature of the free choice open to him and his place in the order of things. The power of blackness that is so conspicuous an element in the literature of the tragic vision paradoxically bears witness to the human passion for truth, no matter where it leads. To live authentically is, in Existentialist parlance, to live in the full knowledge that each one moves irresistibly toward the death that will destroy all his possibilities of becoming.

In thus venturing to face the truth of being, whatever it may disclose, the writer has already gone some distance beyond the myth of the absurd. By insisting that there is nothing beyond man, he prepares the ground for a tragic counter-affirmation. Even if he is a creature of dust, finite and mortal, he will still endeavor, in the brief interval before the light of life is extinguished, to assert his freedom and live in accordance with the humanistic ideal he has chosen. Having cast off all other-worldly illusions, he is ready to affirm what man alone can affirm: there is only this life, here and now. The only effective antidote against the vision of the absurd is to intensify the revolt of consciousness, to unite against the common enemy—death. The tragic hero rebels, always, as we have seen, in the name of life. He engages in a conflict against powers that are overwhelming, and yet he must oppose them. That is the measure of his greatness of soul, even if he cannot give voice to a heartening affirmation of cosmic order and harmony.

Camus, at the time that he composed *The Stranger*, frankly acknowledged the supremacy of the absurd. His entirely consistent position was that the knowledge of the absurd must be kept steadily in view, not hidden by the legerdemain of supernatural sanctions, and then the natural man is free to choose. Meursault chooses. He values his physical sensations, the privilege of being alive, the luminous play of consciousness. He does not, like Ahab, decide to revolt, but his passiveness is in itself a form of revolt.

He yields to the arbitrary control of a mechanical force which is stronger than his will. Fate rules, even when events seem to be without meaning or purpose. Life is a trap; there is no way out.

In comprehending that this is so, Meursault proves that he is no longer an utterly passive victim; he has been raised above the slough of inauthentic existence. He knows that it is cowardly as well as futile to avert one's gaze from this final disclosure of the total indifference of the mechanical universe. The nothingness which will take all men captive at last is not to be exorcised by prayer or hoodwinked by techniques of evasion. The absurdist hero at least knows that death makes no exceptions and sentences all men indiscriminately to die. In such a contingent and therefore absurd universe, it is a species of madness to introduce the category of guilt. Meursault asserts his human freedom and bears with dignity the fate that is thrust upon him.

Nor can the tragic hero, when brought face to face with a universe that frustrates his all-too-human craving for unity, take refuge in the moral values of his society and age. He cannot overcome the forces of opposition resident in Nature and in his own self. It is absurd to dwell in the domain of the absurd but it is even more absurd to assume that art can offer a way of going beyond it. The tragic writer of our time holds both visions, the negative and the positive, in some sort of aesthetic balance while suspecting that both are illusions. The alchemy of art, however sublime its source of inspiration, cannot resolve the contradictions of existence. The writer can arrive at no existential synthesis, no resolution, that will satisfy the requirements of his skeptical mind. The aesthetic resolution is an imaginative exploration of reality that spurns all attempts to demonstrate the final victory of the moral order. The quest for salvation through art turns out to be only an aesthetic delusion. The writer cannot hope to solve his existential conflicts by dealing with them aesthetically. There is no direct passage way between art and reality.

No body of values can save the world. There is no higher reality beyond the world of experience that is steeped in the absurd. It is even more absurd to maintain that tragic art can say "through faith that behind the Manichaean face there is a deeper reality in God, in whose eyes all absurdities are miraculously resolved." [12] Tragic art never says that. This is obviously the language of faith. The theological deification of the absurd cannot provide the foundation of a tragic aesthetic, "since it cannot be communicated or subjected to dramatic portrayal." [13]

It is the modern novel which offers the best articulation of the tragic spirit, a spirit which, however influenced by the Graeco-Christian heritage, is the record of a radically tansformed sensibility. There has been no failure of nerve. The advent of nihilism in literature is not, as is commonly thought, a defeat of the human spirit. Nihilism in art is actually a contradiction in terms; the labor of incorporating it within a work of art is already indicative of a reaching out toward a goal of transcendence. (When, as in the fiction of Samuel Beckett, the possibiltiy of transcendence is denied, the writer falls short of the tragic vision.) The object of the writer today is not to fashion a new mythology but to establish some order of meaning in the chaos of modern life, without the underpinning of religious values. The scientific tradition will have to be assimilated, thought it will be interpreted in diverse ways congenial to the temperament of the writer. Henceforth the universe will no longer be seen in the image of human desire. The link between man and God, the human and the divine, has been broken. The truths of science have supplanted the absolutes of the past. The old mythological power, whether of the Greek or the Christian world, has been emptied of meaning. Whether the "mythologies" born of the scientific imagination can be utilized to produce tragic works that rival those of the past remains to be seen. One thing is certain: man cannot hope to dominate reality except through the art of tragedy, in which human consciousness protests against the absurdity of existence.

Introduction

1. Erich Fromm, *Escape from Freedom*. New York and Toronto: Rinehart & Company, Inc., 1941, pp. 245–46.

2. In Jacobean tragedy we can observe the emergence of the skeptical attitude, the growing uncertainty as to the nature of man and the universe. (Robert Orenstein, *The Moral Vision of Jacobean Tragedy*. Madison: The University of Wisconsin Press, 1960, p. 4.)

3. As Sacheverell Sitwell declares: "there is no heaven and no hell." In our age of reason "the entire edifice of all the religions is no more than a mirage floating over our heads, and induced by our fear of death." (Sacheverell Sitwell, *Journey to the Ends of Time*. New York: Random House, 1959, I, 9.)

4. Albert Camus, *Resistance, Rebellion and Death*. Translated by Justin O'Brien. New York: Alfred A. Knopf, 1961, p. 229.

5. Murray Krieger draws a useful distinction between tragedy as referring to the literary form and "the tragic vision" as bearing on the psychology of the protagonist, his version of reality. "It is more than a difference between two extant approaches to the tragic. Rather, the second has usurped the very possibility of the first after having been born side by side with it." (Murray Krieger, *The Tragic Vision*. New York: Holt, Rinehart and Winston, 1960, pp. 2–3.)

6. Bertrand Russell wryly concludes his book on *Human Knowledge* with the confession that however valuable empiricism has proved as a method, "all human knowledge is uncertain, inexact, and partial." (Bertrand Russell, *Human Knowledge*. New York: Simon and Schuster, 1948, p. 507.)

7. John Gassner, *Theatre at the Crossroads*. New York: Holt, Rinehart and Winston, 1960, p. 25.

8. *Ibid.*, p. 59.

9. Murray Krieger, *The Tragic Vision*, pp. 14–15.

10. Toby Cole (ed.), *Playwrights on Playwriting*. New York: Hill and Wang, 1960, p. 239.

11. Herbert Weisinger, *Tragedy and the Paradox of the Fortunate Fall*. East Lansing: Michigan State University Press, 1953, p. 271.

12. Michael Hamburger, *Reason and Energy*. New York: Grove Press, Inc., 1957, p. 310.

13. Henry Alonzo Myers, *Tragedy: A View of Life*. Ithaca: Cornell University Press, 1956, p. 100.

14. *Ibid.*, p. 53.

15. According to Gottfried Benn, a writer, even if personally afflicted with the deepest pessimism, "would rise from the abyss by the mere fact that he works. The accomplished work itself is a denial of decay and doom." (Gottfried Benn, *Primal Vision*. Edited by E. B. Ashton. Norfolk, Conn.: New Directions, n. d., p. 210.

1—The Problem of Tragedy in the Twentieth Century

1. William Faulkner, *The Sound and the Fury*. New York: The Modern Library, 1946, p. 194.

2. *Ibid.*, p. 196.

3. Ernest Hemingway, *A Farewell to Arms*. New York: The Modern Library, 1932, p. 350.

4. *Ibid.*

5. Jean Anouilh, *Five Plays*. Translated by Lewis Galantière. New York: Hill and Wang, 1958, p. 24.

6. *Ibid.*

7. A brilliant study of this complex process of transformation is to be found in Geoffrey Clive's *The Romantic Enlightenment*. New York: Meridian Books, Inc., 1960.

8. Rainer Maria Rilke, *Selected Works*. Translated by G. Craig Houston. Norfolk, Conn.: New Directions, 1960, I, 4.

9. The zoological image (man viewed as ant or ape, cockroach or wolf), is frequently employed in modern literature as a means of symbolizing the degrading absurdity of human existence. It appears, with different shadings of irony, in "The Burrow" by Kafka and in *Steppenwolf* by Hermann Hesse. This symbol of zoological transformation serves to shadow forth the existential dichotomies inherent in the nihilistic outlook: the total insignificance of the human species when considered biologically is countered by the need to affirm the self and the importance of life. It reveals the conflict between an enduring spiritual urge toward transcendence, the desire to become like unto God, and the impossibility of ever achieving it within a naturalistic framework of values.

10. Hermann Hesse, *Steppenwolf*. Translated by Basil Creighton. New York: Frederick Ungar Publishing Co., 1957, p. 306.

11. "Indeed, comedy is an essential part of tragedy; you cannot portray the limitations of humanity without stumbling on the absurd." Michael Roberts, *T. E. Hulme*. London: Faber and Faber Ltd., 1938, p. 244.

12. Though Turgenev took credit for coining the term "nihilism," it was used as far back as 1790 by Heinrich Jacobi. (August Closs, *Medusa's Mirror*. London: The Cresset Press, 1957, p. 147.) The term "nihilism" refers not only to the extreme revolutionary doctrine that seeks to overthrow the existing structure of society, but also, and this is the meaning we assign to it in this book, the rejection of the dominant religious and moral beliefs of Western civilization. The whole history of nineteenth- and twentieth-century German literature mirrors this crisis of belief. (*Ibid.*, p. 147.) In Russia, the term was applied in

the early nineteenth century to those writers who refused to abide by any leading principles; they became accusers of the established order. Philosophically, nihilism embraced positivism and cherished the ideal of scientific exactitude. "Atheism and materialism are at once preconditions and logical consequences of nihilist criticism and negation." (Thomas Garrigue Masaryk, *The Spirit of Russia*. Translated by Eden and Cedar Paul. London: George Allen & Unwin Ltd., 1919, II, 72.) In the main, however, Russian nihilism was social and political in character, ignoring the metaphysical implications of nihilism present in Schopenhauer's *The World as Will and Idea*. The Russian nihilist, for all his critical negation, never gave way to despair. He is therefore not included in our analysis of the tragic vision. He makes his appearance, however, as one of the terrorists in Camus's play, *The Just Assassins*.

13. Jean Anouilh, *Five Plays*, p. 24.

14. Albert Camus, *The Rebel*. Translated by Anthony Bower. New York: Alfred A. Knopf, 1954, p. 28. "Rebellion is the common ground on which every man bases his first value. I *rebel*—therefore we *exist*."

15. I. A. Richards, *Principles of Literary Criticism*. New York: Harcourt, Brace & Company, 1924, p. 246.

16. Paul Tillich points out that concepts like evolution and will to power are invested with a mythical character and incorporate an element of the religious mentality. Paul Tillich, "The Religious Symbol," in Rollo May (ed.), *Symbolism in Religion and Literature*. New York: George Braziller, 1960, p. 86.

17. Robinson Jeffers, *The Double Axe and Other Poems*. New York, 1948, p. vii.

18. One English critic declares: "I rather doubt if at any time in history so many ordinary individuals have realized the personal reality of death." (Alex Comfort, "The Exposition of Irresponsibility," in Stefan Schimanski and Henry Treece (eds.), *A New Romantic Anthology*. London: Grey Walls Press, 1949, p. 330.) An anthropologist writes: "Today, a myth of general annihilation like

that of the Twilight of the Gods no longer belongs solely to the domain of the imagination." (Roger Caillois, *Man and the Sacred*. Translated by Meyer Barash. Glencoe, Illinois: The Free Press, 1959, p. 180.) Sacheverell Sitwell, in *Journey to the Ends of Time* (I, 8), broods obsessively on the theme of death. If death is the end of life, then the dead body has as much significance as a dead cat in the gutter.

19. Nada, in *The State of Siege*, is only an allegorical abstraction.

20. Albert Camus, *The Rebel*, p. 30.

21. In the plays of his later period, Eugene O'Neill returned to the theme of struggle against fate, but the outcome in each case is foredoomed. *Long Day's Journey into Night* portrays four characters, defeated by their heritage from the past, who must learn to live without hope. Nothing can save them. Edmund, who most closely resembles Eugene O'Neill, says: "I will always be a stranger who never feels at home, who does not really want and is not wanted, who can never belong, who must always be a little in love with death." (Eugene O'Neill, *Long Day's Journey into Night*. New Haven: Yale University Press, 1956.)

22. Gottfried Benn, *Primal Vision*, pp. 79–80.

23. *Ibid.*, p. 82. This nihilistic manifesto was written in 1937.

24. Una Ellis-Fermor, *The Frontiers of Drama*. London: Methuen & Co. Ltd., 1948, p. 14.

25. D. D. Raphael, *The Paradox of Tragedy*. Bloomington: Indiana University Press, 1960, p. 51.

26. Maxwell Anderson, *The Essence of Tragedy*. Washington, D. C.: Anderson House, 1939, p. 13.

2—*The Kierkegaardian Paradox of the Absurd*

1. In attempting to explain his extraordinary productivity as a religious author, Kierkegaard declares: "I am like a spy in a higher service. . . . I am a spy who in his spying, in learning to know all about conduct and illusions and suspicious characters, all the while he is making in-

spection is himself under the closest inspection." (Sören Kierkegaard, *The Point of View*. Translated by Walter Lowrie. London and New York: Oxford University Press, 1950, p. 87.) Here is a portrait of the religious character serving as a spy in a higher service, himself under the closest inspection, that reminds one of *The Trial* and *The Castle*.

2. Sören Kierkegaard, *Concluding Unscientific Postscript*. Translated by David F. Swenson. Princeton: Princeton University Press, 1941, p. 182.

3. J. Heywood Thomas, *Subjectivity and Paradox*. New York: The Macmillan Company, 1957, p. 77.

4. *Ibid.*, p. 123.

5. Sören Kierkegaard, *Either/Or*. 2 vols. Translated by David F. Swenson and Lillian Marvin Swenson. Princeton: Princeton University Press, 1946, I, 11.

6. *Ibid.*, I, 19.

7. Kierkegaard, *Concluding Unscientific Postscript*, p. 234.

8. Kierkegaard, *Either/Or*, I, 116.

9. *Ibid.*, I, 117.

10. *Ibid.*, I, 118.

11. *Ibid.*, I, 121.

12. Kierkegaard, *Concluding Unscientific Postscript*, p. 234.

13. Kierkegaard had originally intended to preface the book with a prayer but finally decided to omit it because that would have made the work too clearly "edifying." Part of the prayer reads: "Grant that we may each one of us become in good time aware what sickness it is which is the sickness unto death, and aware that we are all suffering from this sickness." (Sören Kierkegaard, *The Sickness unto Death*. Translated by Walter Lowrie. Princeton: Princeton University Press, 1946, p. x.)

14. *Ibid.*, p. 26.

15. *Ibid.*, p. 97.

16. Lawrence Thompson, in *Melville's Quarrel with God*, declares that Melville came to look upon God as the source of all evil, "in short, the 'Original Sinner,' divinely depraved." (Lawrence Thompson, *Melville's Quarrel with*

God. Princeton: Princeton University Press, 1952, p. 6.)

17. Kierkegaard, *Sickness unto Death*, p. 207.

18. *Ibid.*, p. 124.

19. Sören Kierkegaard, *The Journals of Sören Kierge-gaard*. Translated by Alexander Dru. London and New York: Geoffrey Cumberlege, 1951, p. 41.

20. *Ibid.*, p. 47.

21. *Ibid.*, p. 390.

22. Kierkegaard, *Concluding Unscientific Postscript*, pp. 150–51.

23. Faulkner's fiction, Existentialist in tone and texture, could very appropriately, according to one critic, be studied in Kierkegaardian terms: "paradox, the absurd, the concept of dread and the dialectic of despair, man's contradictory nature and precarious situation." But the central Kierkegaardian category of faith is strangely absent. "For in the end . . . the *existential* quality of Faulkner's work is probably closer to Heidegger than to Kierkegaard." (Hyatt H. Waggoner, *William Faulkner*. Lexington: University of Kentucky Press, 1959, pp. 257–58.

24. "The task which has to be proposed to the majority of people in Christendom is: Away from the 'poet'! or away from having a relation to or from having one's life in that (instead of existing)—and to become a Christian!" (Kierkegaard, *The Point of View*, p. 74.)

25. Dorothea Krook adopts this approach. "Every product of the creative imagination is individual or personal— 'subjective'—in so far as it is, and must be, the projection of a personal vision; and it is at the same time thoroughly objective in so far as it has a validity transcending the merely individual and personal." (Dorothea Krook, *Three Traditions of Moral Thought*. Cambridge: The University Press, 1959, pp. 11–12.

3—Two Philosophers of the Tragic

1. Camus, *The Rebel*, p. 58.

2. "Schopenhauer's will is in no way different from Melville's and Joyce's vision of God as the maw of univer-

sal death. It anticipates the view of nature fostered by Darwinism. It underlies much of Existentialism. Ultimate reality is without meaning for human existence." (Walter H. Sokel, *The Writer in Extremis*. Stanford: Stanford University Press, 1959, pp. 24–25.)

3. This is but a step removed from the belief that the artist, a priest of the eternal imagination, as Joyce phrases it, transmuting the daily bread of experience into the radiant body of everliving life, is a God unto himself, autonomous and self-sufficient. "The artist, like the God of the creation, remains within or behind or beyond or above his handiwork, invisible, refined out of existence, indifferent, paring his fingernails." (James Joyce, *A Portrait of the Artist as a Young Man*. New York. The Modern Library, 1916, p. 252.)

4. Friedrich Nietzsche, *The Birth of Tragedy*. Translated by Francis Goffing. Garden City, New York: Doubleday and Company, 1956, p. 10.

5. *Ibid.*, p. 11.

6. *The Bacchae*, by Euripides, introduces Dionysus, a newcomer to Mount Olympus, who illustrates the complex nature of the gods, their lack of moral judgment. Teiresias defends the new god of chthonic ecstasy. The blind prophet foregoes his reason, his belief in moderation, and finds himself overcome by impulses that rise from the Dionysian depths. (See R. F. Winnington-Ingram, *Euripides and Dionysus*. Cambridge: The University Press, 1948.)

7. Nietzsche, *The Birth of Tragedy*, p. 23.

8. Walter Kaufman, *Nietzsche*. New York: Meridian Books, 1956, p. 86.

9. Catherine Barclay's dying words are: "I'm not a bit afraid. It's just a dirty trick." (Ernest Hemingway, *A Farewell to Arms*, p. 354.)

10. Karl Jaspers, *Existentialism and Humanism*. Translated by E. E. Ashton. New York: Russell F. Moore Company, 1952, p. 66.

11. "There is no common Western world any more, no deity jointly believed in, no valid image of man, no source

of solidarity throughout all antagonisms, even a fight to the death." (*Ibid.*, p. 80.)

12. Karl Jaspers, *Way to Wisdom*. Translated by Ralph Manheim. New Haven, Conn.: Yale University Press, 1951, p. 38.

13. Karl Jaspers, *Tragedy Is Not Enough*. Translated by Harald A. T. Reiche, Harry T. Moore, and Karl W. Deutsch. Boston: The Beacon Press, 1952, pp. 38–39.

14. *The Metamorphosis of the Gods*, by André Malraux, traces in the historic evolution of art forms the process by which gradually the divine was appropriated by the human.

15. Jaspers, *Tragedy Is Not Enough*, p. 51, declares: "Compared with the transcendent, all is finite and relative, and therefore deserves to be destroyed, the exception as well as the rule."

16. *Ibid.*, p. 75.

17. *Ibid.*, p. 101.

18. *Ibid.*, p. 97.

19. Paul Arthur Schilpp (ed.), *The Philosophy of Karl Jaspers*. New York: Tudor Publishing Company, 1957, p. 832.

20. Jaspers, *Tragedy Is Not Enough*, p. 105.

4—The Nihilistic Universe of Kafka

1. Gunther Anders, *Franz Kafka*. Translated by A. Steer and A. K. Thorlby. London: Bowes & Bowes, 1960, p. 74.

2. Geoffrey Clive, who interprets Kafka's short stories from a Kierkegaardian perspective, declares: "One of the principal paradoxes of the twentieth century is the simultaneous manifestation of great scientific achievement and enormous metaphysical failure." (*The Romantic Enlightenment*, p. 187.)

3. Max Brod (ed.), *The Diaries of Franz Kafka: 1910–1912*. Translated by Joseph Kresh. New York: Schocken Books, 1948, p. 298.

4. André Gorz, *The Traitor*. Translated by Richard

Howard. New York: Simon and Schuster, 1959, p. 223.

5. *Ibid.*, p. 201.

6. Max Brod (ed.), *The Diaries of Franz Kafka*, p. 259.

7. Compare this imaginative bodying forth of the feeling of dread with Kierkegaard's psychological analysis of subjective dread: "the nothing which is the object of dread becomes, as it were, more and more a something." (Sören Kierkegaard, *The Concept of Dread.* Translated by Walter Lowrie. Princeton: Princeton University Press, 1946, p. 55.

8. Gunther Anders, in his study of Kafka as the "poet" of alienation, declares that the reason for this disintegration of the self is simple: "the self which Kafka finds turns out to be an 'alien' self, a stranger with no *raison d'etre* in this world and therefore no being." *Franz Kafka*, p. 20.) The disintegration of the alien self, its loss of being, is a negative expression of one pole of the tragic vision: its fixation on the specter of the absurd.

9. If reality shadows forth only the phantasmagoria of the meaningless, then this would account for the unfinished character of Kafka's work. It would explain, too, the internal structure of his fiction, which is seemingly without the formal order and unity of a plot. The movement to abolish the plot is an outgrowth of the realization of the utter meaninglessness of existence. The hero in Kafka's "absurd" universe is moved about in a "game" which conforms to no conceivable rules; there is no "logical" line of progression in the flow of the narrative. The same condition of "arrest" or stasis is to be found in Samuel Beckett's fiction, where travel, flight, and sensuality are but frantic and futile efforts to escape the fate of meaninglessness. Like Kafka's "fables," Beckett's novels do not end; they simply come to a sudden halt. Freedom of will is an illusion. The riddle of life cannot be solved.

10. "In this mechanized and bureaucratic world, K. is as close as Kafka dare get to an Ivan. It is a world in which heroism is so reduced in strength and stature that this piece of machinery, this cipher, this nonentity clerk,

victim as he is abuser of hierarchy, must become our most satanic representative." (Murray Krieger, *The Tragic Vision*, p. 144.)

11. A number of influential critics like Max Brod, Edwin Muir, Ronald Gray, and Rebecca West maintain that Kafka's work, however ambiguously stylized, is instinct with religious overtones of meaning. The truth is otherwise. Though Kafka uses situations that can be construed in terms of religious concepts, he never leaves the scene of this world, which is mysterious enough in all conscience. He makes no reference to the higher truths of religion. The hunger for transcendence is unmistakably present, but the belief that it can be satisfied has perished. Unlike Kierkegaard, Kafka the metaphysical seeker is not to be distinguished from Kafka the artist. His religious sensibility, as it manifests itself in his fiction, is almost indistinguishable, as Gunther Anders correctly points out, from his literary sensibility, "and this belongs unmistakably to a tradition which has long been religiously 'emancipated' if not outspokenly atheistic." (Gunther Anders, *Franz Kafka*, p. 70.) It is this tradition which provides one of the leading sources of conflict in the complex structure of the modern tragic vision.

12. Rebecca West, *The Court and the Castle*. New Haven: Yale University Press, 1957, p. 301.

13. Kafka writes: "Ever since I can remember I was so concerned about the problem of defending my spiritual existence that everything else was indifferent to me." (Max Brod, *Franz Kafka*. Translated by G. Humphreys Roberts. New York: Schocken Books, 1947, p. 25.)

14. Ronald Gray, *Kafka's Castle*. Cambridge: The University Press, 1956, p. 122.

15. Gunther Anders, *Franz Kafka*, p. 82.

16. *Ibid.*, p. 74.

17. J. P. Hoodin, *The Dilemma of Being Modern*. London: Routledge, 1956, p. 7.

18. Max Brod, *Franz Kafka*, p. 75.

19. "Nowhere does one discern the revolt of Promethean characters against the stupid working of stupid na-

ture, of blind fate; nowhere the healthy, foolhardy rebellion of the 'I' against the 'must.' " (Angel Flores [ed.],
The Kafka Problem. New York: New Directions, 1946,
p. 211.)

5—Albert Camus and the Revolt Against the Absurd

1. Camus, *Resistance, Rebellion and Death*, p. 28.

2. A number of modern dramatists have done so,
among them Jean Anouilh, Gide, Sartre, Cocteau, and
O'Neill.

3. John Cruikshank, *Albert Camus and the Literature
of Revolt*. London and New York: Oxford University
Press, 1959, p. 192.

4. It seemed to him "that man must exalt justice in
order to fight against eternal injustice, create happiness in
order to protest against the universe of unhappiness."
(Camus, *Resistance, Rebellion and Death*, p. 28.)

5. Camus declares: "No, everything is not summed up
in negation and absurdity. We know this. But we must
first posit negation and absurdity because they are what
our generation has encountered and what we must take
into account." (*Ibid.*, p. 59.) On these grounds he repels
the charge that he is an unregenerate nihilist. "After all,
that is why I am an artist, because even the work that
negates still affirms something and does homage to the
wretched and magnificent life that is ours." (*Ibid.*, p. 239.)

6. *Ibid.*, p. 28.

7. Cruikshank, *Camus and the Literature of Revolt*,
p. 57.

8. *The Education of Henry Adams* should be read in
conjunction with our attempt to disentangle the conflicts
and contradictions that make up the ambiguous structure
of the modern tragic vision. Though the old formulas had
failed, as Henry Adams knew, he would not abandon the
quest for meaning. "Every man with self-respect enough
to become effective, if only as a machine, has had to account for himself somehow, and to invent a formula of his
own for his universe, if the standard formulas failed."

(Henry Adams, *The Education of Henry Adams*. Boston and New York: Houghton Mifflin Company, 1918, p. 472.)

9. Albert Camus, *The Myth of Sisyphus*. Translated by Justin O'Brien. New York: Alfred A. Knopf, 1955, p. 31.

10. Albert Camus, *The Stranger*. Translated by Stuart Gilbert. New York: Alfred A. Knopf, 1946, p. 127.

11. *Ibid.*, pp. 151–52.

12. Jean-Paul Sartre, *Literary and Philosophical Essays*. Translated by Annette Michelson. London: Rider & Co., 1955, p. 29.

13. Albert Camus, *Caligula and Three Other Plays*. Translated by Stuart Gilbert. New York: Alfred A. Knopf, 1958, p. vi.

14. *Ibid.*, p. 40.

15. *Ibid.*, p. 42.

16. *Ibid.*, p. 72.

17. Camus, *The Rebel*, p. 16.

18. Albert Camus, *The Plague*. Translated by Stuart Gilbert. New York: Alfred A. Knopf, 1948, pp. 117–18.

6—The Tragic Hero

1. *Hamlet*, II, ii, 313–17.

2. "For remember the larger beasts of prey are *noble* creatures, perfect of their kind." (Oswald Spengler, *Hour of Decision*. Translated by Charles F. Atkinson. New York: Alfred A. Knopf, 1934, p. 21.

3. Viktor E. Frankl, *From Death-Camp to Existentialism*. Translated by Ilse Lasch. Boston: Beacon Press, 1959, p. 99.

4. When life in the Warsaw Ghetto was drawing to a ghastly close, the surviving Jews discussed the crucial issue of what to say if someone could be smuggled out as a messenger. "Everyone agreed that the most important thing was to arouse the world to the horror of the organized extermination we are now suffering." (Emmanuel Ringelblum, *Notes from the Warsaw Ghetto*. Translated by

Jacob Sloan. New York and London: McGraw-Hill Book Co., 1958, p. 291.) These men who were about to perish still preserved their faith in the conscience of mankind. But if the world outside knew what was taking place in the Warsaw Ghetto, it kept strangely silent.

5. *The Black Book*, a study of spiritual etiolation, was written "because today we are among the dead; and this is agon for the dead." (Lawrence Durrell, *The Black Book*. New York: E. P. Dutton & Co., Inc., 1960, p. 22.

6. E. A. Havelock, *The Crucifixion of Intellectual Man*. Boston: Beacon Press, 1951, p. 38.

7. Camus, *Resistance, Rebellion and Death*, p. 266.

8. See "What Is Oblomovschina?" in N. A. Dobrolyubov, *Selected Philosophical Essays*. Translated by J. Fineberg. Moscow: Foreign Language Publishing House, 1948, pp. 174–217.

9. Ernest Hemingway, *A Farewell to Arms*, p. 350.

10. Gottfried Benn, *Primal Vision*, p. 129.

11. Paul Bowles, *Let It Come Down*. New York: Random House, 1952, p. 156.

12. *Ibid.*, p. 222.

13. Paul Bowles, *The Spider's House*, New York: Random House, 1955, p. 195.

14. *Ibid.*, p. 196.

15. In "Novel of the Phenotype," Gottfried Benn pointed out that interest in the existential spells the death of the novel. "Why bother to infuse thoughts into someone, into a figure, into invented personalities, now when there are no longer any personalities? Why invent persons, names, and relationships, just when they begin to be of no account?" (*Primal Vision*, pp. 121–22.)

7—The Tragic Vision and the Scientific Synthesis

1. Joseph Needham, *Man a Machine*. New York: W. W. Norton & Co., 1928, p. 18.

2. Kenneth Burke points out in *Counter-Statement*: "For if tragedy is a sense of man's intimate participation in processes beyond himself, we find that science has re-

placed the older metaphysical structure with an historical structure which gives the individual man ample grounds to feel such participation. What science has taken away from us as a personal relationship to the will of Providence, it has re-given as a personal relationship to the slow, unwieldy movements of human society." (Charles I. Glicksberg (ed.), *American Literary Criticism.* New York: Hendricks House, 1951, p. 322.)

3. Stephen E. Toulmin, Ronald W. Hepburn, and Alasdair Macintyre, *Metaphysical Beliefs.* London: SCM Press Ltd., 1957, p. 28.

4. "He lost his faith in the traditional illogical concept of a benign god and of a personal immortality, and he accepted with stoicism a monistic concept in which God, the Immanent Will or It, as he preferred to think of it, was neither loveless nor hateless but was a blind power creating without concept of what it was doing. With these ideas, he had formulated a personal philosophy which permitted him to accept life as it came." (James Granville Southworth, *The Poetry of Thomas Hardy.* New York: Columbia University Press, 1947, p. 228.)

5. J. O. Bailey, *Thomas Hardy and the Cosmic Mind.* Chapel Hill: The University of North Carolina Press, 1956, pp. 93–94.

6. George Steiner, *The Death of Tragedy.* New York: Alfred A. Knopf, 1961, p. 353.

7. Opposed to the doctrine of empathy, as Worringer points out, is an aesthetic system which is rooted in man's urge to abstraction. It arises from a characteristically different *Weltanschauung.* "Whereas the precondition for the urge to empathy is a happy pantheistic relationship of confidence between man and the phenomena of the external world, the urge to abstraction is the outcome of a great inner unrest inspired in man by the phenomena of the outside world. . . . We might describe this state as an immense spiritual dread of space." (Wilhelm Worringer, *Abstraction and Empathy.* Translated by Michael Bullock. London: Routledge & Kegan Paul, 1953, p. 15.)

8. Gottfried Benn, *Primal Vision*, p. 102.

9. Alfred North Whitehead, *Science and the Modern World*. New York: The Macmillan Company, 1948, p. 16.

10. D. H. Lawrence, *Fantasia of the Unconscious*. New York: Thomas Seltzer, 1922, p. 218.

11. Everett W. Knight, *Literature Considered as Philosophy*. London: Routledge & Kegan Paul, 1957, p. 42.

12. Arthur Hobson Quinn, *A History of the American Drama from the Civil War to the Present Day*. 2 vols. New York: F. S. Crofts & Co., 1945, II, 199.

13. This is pointed out by Doris V. Falk, in *Eugene O'Neill and the Tragic Focus*. New Brunswick: Rutgers University Press, 1958, pp. 34–35.

14. Eugene O'Neill, *Nine Plays*. New York: The Modern Library, 1952, p. 523.

15. *Ibid.*, p. 680.

8—*Psychoanalysis and the Tragic Vision*

1. Though literary artists are deeply influenced by the intellectual systems of their age, they need not, of course, include them within their work.

2. See the chapter on "Precursors of Freud," in Frederick J. Hoffman, *Freudianism and the Literary Mind*. New York: Grove Press, 1959, pp. 297–313.

3. Lionel Trilling rightly disputes Thomas Mann's contention that Freud sought to legitimize the dark irrational contents of the psyche. "On the contrary, his rationalism supports all the ideas of the Enlightenment that deny validity to myth or religion; he holds to a simple materialism, to a simple determinism, to a rather limited sort of epistemology." (Lionel Trilling, *The Liberal Imagination*. New York: The Viking Press, 1950, p. 41.)

4. For the various uses of and reactions against Freudian ideas see William York Tindall, *Forces in Modern British Literature*. New York: Alfred A. Knopf, 1947, pp. 318–59.

5. See "Freud and Jung," in Melvin J. Friedman, *Stream of Consciousness*. New Haven: Yale University Press, 1955, pp. 99–120.

6. See "Psycho-analysis and the Problem of Aesthetic Value," in Herbert Read, *The Forms of Things Unknown*. New York: Horizon Press, 1960, pp. 76–93.

7. Sigmund Freud, *Collected Papers*. Translated by James Strachey. London: International Psycho-analytical Press, 1950, I, 208.

8. Sigmund Freud, *New Introductory Lectures on Psychoanalysis*. Translated by W. J. H. Sprott. New York: W. W. Norton & Co., 1933, pp. 228–29.

9. Jung, by way of contrast, early recognized that the sickness and suffering of the individual is not to be explained in terms of neuroses. On the contrary, what they betray is his lack of values. Jung also denied that human destiny is governed by the faculty of reason.

10. Sigmund Freud, *New Introductory Lectures on Psychoanalysis*. Translated by W. J. H. Sprott. New York: W. W. Norton & Co., 1933, p. 112.

11. Paul Federn, "The Reality of the Death Instinct," *Psychoanalytic Review*, XIX (1932), 143.

12. A number of modern works utilize this symbolic motif in their title: *Journey to the End of the Night* by Céline, *Long Day's Journey into Night* by O'Neill, *Journey to the Ends of Time* by Sacheverell Sitwell, and many others. See Maud Bodkin, *Archetypal Patterns in Poetry*. London: Oxford University Press, 1934. Jung discusses the function of the archetypes in *Psychological Types*. Translated by H. Godwin Baynes. New York: Harcourt, Brace & Company, Inc., 1926, p. 476. In *The Psychology of the Unconscious*, Jung studies the primordial images which are the most ancient and universal thoughts of mankind.

13. One critic holds that Sartre's free choice resembles Freudian psychological determinism rather than "free will" that is exercised as the result of a rational decision. (See Nathan N. Green, *Jean-Paul Sartre*. Ann Arbor: University of Michigan Press, 1960, p. 171.) But what Sartre as dramatist and novelist emphasizes is the power of the authentic individual to act as if he were free. Orestes, the hero of *The Flies*, is actually free.

14. Jean-Paul Sartre, *Existential Psychoanalysis*. Trans-

lated by Hazel E. Barnes. New York: Philosophical Library, 1953, p. 234.

15. Rollo May, Ernest Engel, and Henri F. Ellenberger (eds.), *Existence*. New York: Basic Books, 1958, p. 120.

16. *Ibid.*, p. 145.

17. Existential analysis frankly acknowledges its debt of insight to literature, especially to Tolstoy's "The Death of Ivan Ilyitch."

18. Toby Cole (ed.), *Playwrights on Playwriting*, p. 182.

19. Eric Bentley, *The Playwright as Thinker*. New York, 1947, p. 63.

20. Herbert Read, *The Forms of Things Unknown*, p. 186.

21. Eugene O'Neill, *All God's Chillun Got Wings* and *Welded*. New York: Boni and Liveright, 1924, p. 151.

22. W. David Sievers, *Freud on Broadway*. New York: Hermitage House, 1955, p. 98.

23. The only life, as Nina Leeds perceives, "is in the past and future. . . . the present is an interlude . . . strange interlude in which we call on past and future to bear witness we are living!" (Eugene O'Neill, *Nine Plays*, p. 646.)

24. "In other words, whereas O'Neill seems to be saying, 'See, human nature has not changed!' Sartre is launching a violent attack on Aeschylus." (Hazel B. Barnes, *The Literature of Possibility*. Lincoln: University of Nebraska Press, 1959, p. 21.)

25. Eugene O'Neill, *Nine Plays*, p. 759.

26. *Ibid.*, p. 862.

27. *Ibid.*, pp. 866–67.

9—*Existentialism and the Tragic Vision*

1. Jean-Paul Sartre, *Baudelaire*. Translated by Martin Turnell. Norfolk, Conn.: New Directions, 1950, p. 71.

2. "Existential psychoanalysis rejects all determinism —biological, psychological, environmental." (Hazel E. Barnes, *The Literature of Possibility*, p. 282.)

3. André Gorz, *The Traitor*, pp. 37–38.

4. *Ibid.*, p. 180.

5. Jean-Paul Sartre, *Being and Nothingness*. Translated by Hazel E. Barnes. New York: Philosophical Library, 1956, p. lxvi.

6. Fyodor Dostoevski, *The Possessed*. Translated by Constance Garnett. New York: The Macmillan Company, 1916, p. 105.

7. Jean-Paul Sartre, *Existentialism*. Translated by Bernard Frechtman. New York: Philosophical Library, 1947, pp. 60–61.

8. Jean-Paul Sartre, *Nausea*. Translated by Lloyd Alexander. Norfolk, Conn.: New Directions, 1949, p. 171.

9. Jean-Paul Sartre, *The Reprieve*. Translated by Eric Sutton. New York: Alfred A. Knopf, 1947, pp. 363–364.

10. Jean-Paul Sartre, *Troubled Sleep*. Translated by Gerard Hopkins. New York: Alfred A. Knopf, 1951, p. 86.

11. In his discussion of *The Flies*, Robert Champigny declares that the revelation of freedom "is not tragic in itself. It may become tragic if one sees it against the overwhelming background of being, of nature, or other freedoms." (Robert Champigny, *Stages on Sartre's Way*. Bloomington: Indiana University Press, 1959, p. 88.) Orestes illustrates the Sartrean thesis that man is born without his will into the world but must invent his own values. Champigny calls *The Flies* a "pure" form of tragedy. (*Ibid.*, p. 93.)

12. Jean-Paul Sartre, *No Exit*. Translated by Stuart Gilbert. New York: Alfred A. Knopf, 1947, p. 38.

13. *Ibid.*, p. 58.

14. *Ibid.*, p. 58.

15. Jean-Paul Sartre, *The Devil and the Good Lord*. Translated by Kitty Black. New York: Alfred A. Knopf, 1960, p. 13.

16. *Ibid.*, pp. 34–35.

17. *Ibid.*, p. 55.

18. *Ibid.*, p. 61.

19. *Ibid.*, p. 112.

20. *Ibid.*, p. 124.

21. *Ibid.*, p. 140.

22. *Ibid.*, p. 141.

23. *Ibid.*, p. 143.

24. *Ibid.*, p. 149.

25. Jean-Paul Sartre, *The Condemned of Altona.* Translated by Sylvia and George Leeson. New York: Alfred A. Knopf, 1961, p. 165.

26. *Ibid.*, p. 178.

27. *Ibid.*, p. 178.

28. Simone de Beauvoir, *The Ethics of Ambiguity.* Translated by Bernard Frechtman. New York: Philosophical Library, 1948, pp. 12–13.

10—Tragedy and the Marxist Synthesis

1. Friedrich Engels writes: "Men make their own history, whatever its outcome may be, in that each person follows his own consciously desired ends, and it is precisely the resultant of these many wills operating in different directions and of their manifold effects upon the outer world that constitutes history. Thus it is also a question of what the many individuals desire. The will is determined by passion or deliberation. But the levers which immediately determine pasion or deliberation are of very different kinds. Partly they may be external objects, partly ideal motives, ambitions, 'enthusiasm for truth and justice,' personal hatreds or even purely individual whims of all kinds. But, on the other hand, we have seen that the many individual wills active in history for the most part produce results quite other than they intended; quite the opposite; their motives therefore in relation to the total result are likewise only of secondary interest." Friedrich Engels, *Ludwig Feuerbach and the Outcome of Classical German Philosophy.* Edited by C. P. Dutt. New York, n. d., pp. 58–59.

2. George V. Plekhanov, *Art and Society.* Translated by Paul Leitner, Alfred Goldstein, and C. H. Crout. New York, 1936, p. 54.

3. See George Gibian, *Interval of Freedom*, Minneapolis: The University of Minnesota Press, 1960, pp. 20–22.

4. Joseph Needham, *History Is on Our Side*. New York: The Macmillan Co., 1947, p. 10.

5. George Thomson, *Aeschylus and Athens*. London: Lawrence and Wishart, 1941, pp. 158–59.

6. Christopher Caudwell, *Illusion and Reality*. New York: International Publishers, 1938, p. 50.

7. *Ibid.*, pp. 324–25.

8. N. G. Chernyshevsky, *Selected Philosophical Essays*. Moscow: Foreign Language Publishing House, 1953, p. 380.

9. Rufus W. Mathewson, *The Positive Hero in Russian Literature*. New York: Columbia University Press, 1959, p. 100.

10. *Ibid.*, p. 101.

11. John Willett, *The Theatre of Bertold Brecht*. London: Methuen & Co., 1959, p. 77.

12. Bertold Brecht, *Seven Plays*. Edited by Eric Bentley. New York: Grove Press, Inc., 1961, p. 1.

13. Gottfried Benn, *Primal Vision*, p. 41.

14. *Ibid.*, p. 42.

15. Irving Howe, *Politics and the Novel*. New York: Horizon Press, 1957, p. 63.

16. Albert Camus, *The Possessed*. Translated by Justin O'Brien. New York: Alfred A. Knopf, 1960, p. vi.

17. Fyodor Dostoevski, *The Possessed*, p. 377.

18. *Ibid.*, p. 391.

19. *Ibid.*, p. 391.

20. *Ibid.*, p. 391.

21. *Ibid.*, p. 543.

22. *Ibid.*, p. 636.

23. Albert Camus, *The Rebel*, p. 218.

24. Albert Camus, *Caligula and Other Plays*, p. 221.

25. Albert Camus, *Resistance, Rebellion and Death*, p. 179.

26. Albert Camus, *Caligula and Other Plays*, p. 260.

11—Existentialism Versus Marxism

1. John Lewis, *Marxism and the Open Mind*. London: Routledge & Kegan Paul, 1957, p. 172.

2. Georg Lukacsz, "Existentialism," in Roy Wood Sellars, V. J. McGill, and Marvin Farber (eds.), *Philosophy for the Future*. New York: The Macmillan Co., 1940, p. 580.

3. Roger Garaudy, *Literature of the Graveyard*. Translated by Joseph M. Bernstein. New York: International Publishers, 1948, p. 15.

4. Simone de Beauvoir, *The Ethics of Ambiguity*, p. 9.

5. Jean-Paul Sartre, *The Devil and the Good Lord*, p. 386.

6. Champigny points out that Sartre's theater "owes its powerful appeal to tragic irony, to the harsh conflict between masked freedoms, between personal and social morals, between means and ends." (Robert Champigny, *Stages on Sartre's Way*, p. 177.)

7. Jean-Paul Sartre, *What Is Literature?*. Translated by Bernard Frechtman. New York: Philosophical Library, 1949, p. 250 n.

8. André Gorz, *The Traitor*, pp. 206–7.

9. "The absolute in history is for Sartre the human condition, while for the Marxist the absolute is the economic base in its evolutionary forms." (Nathan N. Greene, *Jean-Paul Sartre*, p. 142.)

12—Malraux and the Myth of Violence

1. A. Robert Caponigri, *Time and Idea*. London: Routledge and Kegan Paul, Ltd., 1953, p. 92.

2. André Malraux, *The Conquerors*. Translated by Winifred Stephen Whale. New York: Harcourt, Brace & Co., 1929, p. 103.

3. The same motif is sounded in the *The Grapes of Wrath* and *In Dubious Battle*. It is embodied also, with some sentimental exaggerations, in the character of Prewitt in *From Here to Eternity*.

4. André Malraux, *Man's Fate*. Translated by Haakon M. Chevalier. New York: The Modern Library, 1924, p. 12.

5. *Ibid.*, p. 59.

6. *Ibid.*, p. 241.

7. *Ibid.*, p. 306.
8. *Ibid.*, p. 321.
9. *Ibid.*, p. 323.
10. *Ibid.*, p. 323.
11. Roger Garaudy, *Literature of the Graveyard*, p. 35.
12. *Ibid.*, p. 35.
13. Gerda Blumenthal, *Andre Malraux*. Baltimore: The Johns Hopkins Press, 1960, p. 120.

13—Conclusion

1. "I believe that this *nada* as used by Hemingway is basically the Nothingness of the existentialists, the strange, unknowable, impending threat of nihilation, the *Nichts* of Heidegger, the *néant* of Sartre, and the nada of Unamuno." (John Killinger, *Hemingway and the Dark Gods*. Lexington: University of Kentucky Press, 1960, p. 15.)
2. Arthur Koestler, *Insight and Outlook*. New York: The Macmillan Company, 1949, p. 380.
3. Hermann Diem, *Kierkegaard's Dialectic of Existence*. Translated by Harold Knight. Edinburgh and London: Oliver and Boyd, 1959, p. 442.
4. Sören Kierkegaard, *Concluding Unscientific Postcript*, p. 448.
5. *Ibid.*, p. 450.
6. Sören Kierkegaard, *The Journal of Sören Kierkegaard*, p. 59.
7. Martin Heidegger, *An Introduction to Metaphysics*. Translated by Ralph Manheim. New Haven: Yale University Press, 1959, pp. 5–6.
8. *Ibid.*, p. 4.
9. Eugene O'Neill, *Nine Plays*, p. 336.
10. *Ibid.*, p. 337.
11. *Ibid.*, p. 339.
12. Murray Krieger, *The Tragic Vision*, p. 265.
13. *Ibid.*, p. 266.

INDEX